Diary of a Good Christian Girl

Jules Green

ARK house

Ark House Press
arkhousepress.com

Cataloguing in Publication Data:
Title: Diary Of A Good Christian Girl
ISBN: 978-0-6453714-5-1 (pbk)
Subjects: REL012170 [RELIGION / Christian Living / Personal Memoirs]; REL012070 [RELIGION / Christian Living / Personal Growth]; PSY002000 [PSYCHOLOGY / Developmental / Adolescent];

Design by initiateagency.com

TABLE OF CONTENTS

PREFACE

Within these pages are some very painful and difficult memories. I hope the story of my darkest times will encourage others to speak their stories, their truths, and to know that they are not alone.

I have included a list of resources and helplines for trauma survivors at the back of this book.

Names have been changed for safety purposes, as have several place names.

The Journey to Freedom, Finding Myself

Here I am, the great warrior princess in action. It took me a long time to find myself anew.

As a child, I received some insights into who God made me to be, and the training and teaching I received from my awesome parents really helped.

My childhood was one of healthy exploration, of acting on my intuition to help others by using my already present gifts of prayer and spiritual dreams, and my deep desire to protect others. It was a happy childhood full of love.

But then my warrior essence was squashed, and I was moulded into an unhealthy fantasy of who a good Christian woman should be.

I was confused about myself for many years, burying my trauma, trying to fit into a box that was way too small for me, dulling myself down so others less true to themselves didn't feel intimidated.

But then I remembered ...

Not just the trauma but the warrior within! I began to be true to her, the great warrior princess, and now my life will never be the same.

I have returned to the truth of who God made me. No longer will I be afraid to be the warrior, despite the cultural pressure to conform to our society's ideals for women – submissive, non-confrontational, pleasant, nice, invisible.

But who wants a warrior who isn't fierce? Who wants a warrior who can't fight? I can't be the "nice" girl anymore. "Nice girl" said like that just means compliant, and I can't be true to who God made me if I squash myself into that box. My purpose is clear: Fight for truth, protect others, be a voice for those unable to speak.

I will be the warrior! From now on, I remain unapologetically me.

ACT 1

The Warrior Emerges

The orchestra plays Grieg's morning, signifying a brand new day. The music swells and the young warrior princess sings the beginnings of her story...

CHAPTER 1

Early Childhood

I was born in Sydney to two loving parents. I am the second beautiful daughter. My older sister, Breanna, is two years my senior. We played well together and have always got on.

Eight years after my birth, Candace, the cheeky life of the party, arrived. She was, and still is, a great joy to all who meet her. There is no one like Candace to get a party going, but also to ensure it stays a positive, safe atmosphere. When she was a teenager, she used to sneak out of her room to go and comfort and counsel her friends when they were down. Yes, to comfort, not to get drunk or go to parties.

Early on it became evident to Mum and Dad that I was talented in the arts. I was always drawing and some of my drawings were quite good for a tiny tot. Mum also noticed that I could sing along to songs accurately, remembering the words and getting every note right. They nurtured my creative talents throughout the years, spending thousands of dollars on art materials, paying for design courses and singing weekends, and always encouraging me in any creative endeavours.

I was an early smiler. Mum says I began smiling at two weeks. Even though the nurses told her it was just gas, she knew it was a genuine smile, because I looked right at her and smiled in happy recognition. A mother's love will make you smile.

I've always liked telling silly jokes and making people laugh. I remember sometimes my family would laugh at me because I'd said something funny. For a while I would get upset and say, "I'm not funny!" I thought they meant peculiar. Finally, I realised they meant that I made them laugh and that it was a good thing.

My whole family has a good sense of humour. Dad continues to tell silly stories and make silly comments, now to his grandchild, my son Bree. He also invents silly games. Something he's very good at is using humour to speak into people's lives. Mum, on the other hand, is sarcastic and responds to that type of humour.

My parents were very loving and attentive, always watching over us and looking after us. Mum often came to school excursions with us, and she was the primary carer and homemaker. Some people got their noses out of joint about that, thinking she should have been working, or that Dad wasn't letting her work. In reality, being the stay-at-home mum was her choice. Dad knew better than to tell her to go to work when she didn't want to. Mum is a strong woman with a stubborn streak. You won't make her do something she doesn't want to do.

Dad worked full-time as a clerk for the Australian Defence Department. He also had another, God-ordained, job. One that is more important than any of the other jobs he's had. He is a prophet of God. He has travelled all over Australia and other parts of the world to share his prophetic insights with others.

When we were young, Dad regularly met with his mates to pray in our garage. They'd pray for hours, getting very excited and loud, declaring things and praising God. You could hear them from inside the house with the door closed.

Dad took his role as head of the house seriously. He always watched over the family well and helped us sort out any problems. There was never any violence or unkindness, just parental love done well. He kept the family in order. We kids grew up knowing we could trust our folks and go to them for help, counsel, or just time.

The three sisters got on well and still do. We are great friends and really love each other, there is always a lot of fun play and sibling banter, with a bit of healthy rivalry thrown in.

As a family, we were completely functional. So much so that a lady commented on us one time as we walked along the beach. She was looking at us when she said, "It's beautiful isn't it?" At first, we thought she meant the view. She meant us. We must have been a healthy model of what God intended for families, which is nice to know.

Saying sorry and learning to forgive were big things in our house. Mum and Dad set the tone of being appropriately open. They knew how to admit wrongdoing and say sorry, and we learned how to be humble by example.

There were times when we kids were made to say sorry even when we didn't want to. One day, when I was about six, I had a fight with Breanna. Dad said I needed to say sorry to Breanna and Breanna was to say, "I forgive you", and vice versa. But I got upset about the order we said it in, so the fight started all over again. How ridiculous! We eventually started talking again and enjoyed the rest of our family time.

I remember the first time I gave my heart to the Lord, at age five, during Sunday school. The teacher asked if anyone wanted to invite Jesus into their heart. I said, "yes" and the teacher prayed a simple prayer for me. I was only five, so obviously I didn't understand my decision the way an adult or even an older child would. I just knew I wanted it. I wanted to be friends with Jesus. I could feel that pull towards him, the allure of his great love, and I knew he was calling me to himself. Mum and Dad were so proud and happy when I told them.

Most of my early childhood memories are positive: playing, picnics in parks, feeding ducks, time with family – normal childhood memories. There is, however, one negative memory that has stayed with me.

We were living in a flat in Bankstown, right next to a playground. One evening, I realised I'd left my favourite teddy at the park. It was a home-made cloth teddy bear. The type where the features are printed onto the fabric, then the bear is stuffed and sewn together. Mum had made him for me.

Mum went to the park to retrieve the bear, and when she came back, she had to explain that teddy had been slashed with a knife.

She showed me the pieces. Poor teddy was in shreds with all his stuffing hanging out!

I cried and begged Mum to sew him back together but she said she couldn't. He was too damaged. I heard Mum say to Dad, "Fancy doing that to a child's plaything!"

At a recent visit to the psychologist we talked about this incident, and I realised I had felt for years that what happened with teddy had been minimised. I realise now how traumatised I had been.

Breanna's Vision

We shared our flat in Bankstown with a lady called Radiance. She was in her late twenties, close in age to Mum. She had a mane of beautiful auburn curls. We loved her hair. I remember admiring the colour and texture. However, I began to sense that something was wrong with Radiance. Even we kids could tell she needed healing.

One day Breanna ran to take cover behind the dining table, crying out, "Mummy, Mummy, there's a lion chasing Radiance!"

Mum was alarmed and asked Breanna to describe what she had seen. Breanna said it was a mean, scary lion on the prowl, hunting Radiance, with its teeth bared. The Bible says the devil prowls around like a roaring lion looking for someone to devour (1 Peter 5:8). Mum realised the devil was after Radiance. My mother, the warrior, immediately prayed for protection for Radiance and the family and for divine protection over the flat.

I began to notice a good spiritual atmosphere around the family and in the flat too, which I now realise was the Holy Spirit. God was working in our lives, using Mum and Dad's love, care, discernment and wisdom to help heal Radiance of her childhood traumas, which ultimately blessed all of us living there, including us kids. The blessings trickled down.

Later, Mum told me that's why God instructed them to move in with Radiance in the first place – to help heal her.

When Breanna was a baby, Mum and Dad made friends with a couple named Toby and Ruth. We've known them so long, now they are practically family. When Breanna and I were really young, Toby and Ruth had a holiday house on the South

Coast of New South Wales in a little town called Narrawallee. It was a weatherboard house painted a lovely shade of sky blue. We had summer holidays with them and went swimming and body surfing, played board games and explored the local area.

After living in the Bankstown flat for a couple of years, we moved to live with Mum's mum, Grandma Ebony. Grandma had a lovely big garden with a large garden bed next to the garage, containing flowers with popping seed pods. I used to love popping them.

Having sleepovers with Dad's folks was one of our favourite things to do. We loved having Grandpa Story Time! He used to make up the most fabulous tales, about alligators living in the drain, cars that took us to the moon, and him being a part of the "under 15's, all-girls soccer team!" He always made us laugh.

Grandpa liked to dance, and we liked to dance with him. He was also an artist. He made some lovely drawings and paintings, several of which he gave as gifts throughout the years. I liked drawing with him.

My first solid memories of school are from this time, too. I made my best friend, Louana, while living there. Louana and I have been friends for thirty-six years. Now that's an achievement. We've known each other almost our entire lives. We both have the same silly sense of humour. I still laugh about the evening we went to a playground and Louana covered her feet in sand from the sandpit and said, "Look at my sand shoes".

Louana and I did everything together. We played imaginative games at school and saw each other on the weekends. Our favourite game involved pretending the dirt road going through the school was a river. We had to cross the 'river' and save each other from the crocodiles. Sometimes, we played Mary Poppins and sometimes other little girls joined in. It was a friendly class with lovely children.

I was a tomboy, so I often sat with the boys during classes. I was a big, tall, strong girl; taller than most of the boys. I remember playing arm wrestles with the boys. I could beat them all. I was so proud.

CHAPTER 2

A New Arrival

Mum was forty-one when Candace was born. Breanna and I really wanted a baby sister so we asked Dad if he could please let Mummy have another baby. Mum and Dad talked about it, and the next thing I knew, Mum told us she was pregnant! I didn't believe her at first. I said, "You can't be pregnant Mummy, you're not fat!" Mum replied, "I'll get fat."

On the morning Dad told us Mum had given birth to a little girl named Candace, Breanna was so happy she cried.

Mum had to stay in hospital with Candace for about a week, because her blood pressure had gone far too high during the birth and the nurses wanted to keep an eye on her.

Dad cooked while Mum was in hospital. He only knew how to make three meals, so he rotated them for that week. Sometimes we even got dessert. It was good to start with, but by the end of that week we were glad to get Mum's cooking back.

I remember visiting Mum and Candace in hospital. Mum was in bed, talking to her room mates, looking sleepy, and tiny baby Candace was curled up asleep in her cot. She was beautiful! I couldn't believe how tiny she was. I gave Candace the toy lamb Dad helped me buy for her, and she curled her tiny fingers around my index finger. I felt happy. I was a big sister.

Danger Signs

While we were living at Grandma Ebony's, Auntie Amber started dating a strange man, a man I now call Uncle Shark. (I call him that because he's so dangerous. I hear the Jaws theme when I think of him.) Even though she seemed really happy, we all had a bad feeling about him. Grandpa warned Auntie about him, saying that the man didn't respect women.

They hadn't been together long when they announced their engagement. Auntie Amber told us that her priest had warned her not to marry him. But because he'd been turning on the charm for the whole family, we all second-guessed our instincts.

Once they were married, it took less than a year for his true colours to show, and murmurings of his controlling behaviour slipped through to us. But we didn't know what was true or not, so we didn't say anything.

More Good Memories

About a year after living with Grandma Ebony, a tortoiseshell cat turned up on our balcony. She was there each morning for three consecutive days. She had no collar, but Mum told us not to feed her in case the owners were looking for her. Grandma couldn't resist, and fed her milk.

After about four days, Mum allowed us to keep her. We called her Mittens because she had four white paws that contrasted with the rest of her patchy, orange and black coat.

We had Mittens for years. She moved with us twice. She was a friendly, sweet little cat. She'd come and sit on our laps, curl up and purr. She was a blessing.

We had asked Mum if we could have a kitten called Mittens just before she turned up. We even prayed for a tortoise shell cat with white paws. Then, there she was, a walking, breathing, answer to prayer on four legs.

She gave us comfort. When she was ready to die, she left us, going as mysteriously as she'd come.

Once, we travelled to Parks with our church family, to help out on a property owned by some friends. It was a prophetic mission trip combined with a farm working bee. The property owners wanted us to pray over their land, as well as paint the sheds and dig a well. Mum has a great photo of Dad down in the well, wearing a t-shirt that said, "Kicking butt for the Lord!" So Dad!

At night, we sat around the campfire, eating, talking and singing.

We were given fresh milk straight from the cows, and we were allowed to join in with the farm workers morning tea. What a spread was put on for us. Home baked scones with jam and cream, biscuits, hot drinks, buns, savoury muffins, the whole works. That was their way of saying thanks for the help.

Another couple lived on a property nearby, and they often invited us to stay. Their property was beautiful; a big rectangular house with a gardened quadrangle in the centre; tucked into a damp little valley surrounded by forest. I loved their country garden; growing with fruit trees and vegies, with a grassy area covered with moss and decorated with fern trees, and a brook flowing through. I called it the fairy glen. I used to walk down there early in the morning, stand on the little bridge and watch the sunlight glint off the dewdrops.

When Candace was eighteen months old, we moved again to Dad's parents' house in Greens Ville.

While living with Dad's folks, Grandpa Joseph and Grandma Mary, I began having vivid spiritual dreams. Years later, I realised these dreams have meaning. Sometimes they are warnings from God about bad things the devil is planning, other times they are communicating God's plans for people, places or nations, and sometimes they are showing God's desires for me personally. But back then, I didn't know what was happening to me.

I remember going into Mum and Dad's room and asking about those dreams. Dad didn't know as much about gifts of spiritual sight back then, so he didn't know what advice to give me.

I also began sensing an evil presence in the room I shared with Breanna. It often turned up at night and tried to spook me. A few times, I woke up sensing something near me. Once I even felt its breath, and its cold hand touching my arm.

One night, I woke up with a start and felt this terrifying presence once again. I got out of bed, walked up and down the stairs, and began praying in tongues. It was the first time I'd used the gift of tongues to do warfare, and it worked. The spirit stopped hassling me. God is always stronger.

Sure, it was a spooky time, but God used it to grow my gift of spiritual sight, and to teach me discernment. God always takes bad things and uses them for good. Love always wins.

I was baptised at this time in a rock pool at one of the nearby beaches.

CHAPTER 3

The Warrior Confronts Wrongs

My friend Tamarin and her family lived in a huge old house which used to be a boarding school. One year, during Tamarin's birthday party, her older brother told us some ghost stories about the property.

He told us that one of the students tripped down the stairs one night, on his way to the bathroom, and died. He said that every now and then, the boy's ghost would run down the stairs and then disappear, dying all over again.

The next story was about a mean lady teacher who "haunted" the lounge room.

I didn't believe the stories because I had been taught that ghosts aren't real. So I wasn't scared ... until I saw the ghosts.

Later that night, when we were tucked up in our sleeping bags, I awoke suddenly, for no apparent reason. I sat straight up in my sleeping bag and looked at the stairs.

I saw a figure dressed in glowing white run down the stairs. I thought, "What is that? Who is that? Is that the ghost?" Then, "No, it's probably Tamarin's brother, being silly, playing a trick."

I felt calmer saying that to myself, until I saw the figure stop at the bottom of the stairs, then vanish.

I was stunned. "I've just seen a ghost."

I couldn't really believe it, but I couldn't deny what I'd seen. I didn't tell anyone. I didn't really understand. Now I know that it was a bad case of place memory – where a place absorbs the trauma that happened there, and pictures of that trauma replay like a movie over the area it happened in.

Some people can't see it, but those who have the gift of sight can.

The following year I again attended Tamarin's birthday party with the same bunch of girls. The same ghost stories were told by her brother. I started feeling scared and shaky. Tamarin's brother pulled me aside and told me they were just stories. I said, "I've never seen a ghost." When what I wanted to say was, "I saw the little boy from your story! And they're not just stories."

That night I again woke up suddenly and became aware of a malignant presence in the room.

I looked around, checking that my friends were safe. Then I saw her.

She was standing behind one of my sleeping friends, dressed Victorian style, in a red dress worn over petticoats, with a hat on and her hair up in a severe bun. She looked mean and stern. I knew she was evil.

She turned her head to look at me.

I knew it wasn't just my imagination. I started praying for God's protection over my friends. I prayed for a holy bubble to encapsulate us; to surround us so that she couldn't touch or hurt us. I was especially concerned for my friends. I wasn't so worried about myself.

I proclaimed safety and peace over my friends, and the presence left after about half an hour of me praying solidly.

I knew we were safe now. God had saved us.

I'd had the feeling she would have hurt us if God hadn't awoken me, alerted me to the danger, and got me to pray. I can see now that God was using me as a warrior princess and intercessor even then. He used me to get rid of a demon from that house.

Problems at School

Most of my school friends were lovely children. But there were a couple of strange, manipulative girls.

Antonia was a liar and a thief; stealing the special art materials my parents had bought for me, then claiming I'd been the one to steal them from her.

Then there was Aberline, whom the other children warned me about, telling me not to play with her. I wasn't sure how much of what they said was true, and I felt sad for her because she didn't have many friends. So I agreed to play with her when she asked.

I soon found out how manipulative she could be.

She started making a big fuss about my body hair. She'd tell me I had to shave, that boys wouldn't like me if I didn't shave and that women having hair was wrong. I told her I didn't want to shave yet because we were only eleven and I didn't feel ready. I'd only just started growing hair too; it wasn't as if I was Miss Gorilla.

One day I was walking with her and Candace, who wanted to come with me to Aberline's house. On the way there, Aberline kept bullying me to run, saying I had to lose weight. (We were only eleven, the pressure to look a certain way starts really young.)

She wasn't the only one to hassle me about my weight at such a young age. Some of the other children did it too. One girl said, "You need to go on Jenny Craig. When you got in the car the other day, I saw it sink down. You must be really fat!"

Losing weight is not generally recommended for children. Some kids go through a chubby stage as part of their natural growth. If the child is happy and healthy, who cares if they don't look the way society says they should? It isn't healthy for young children, especially girls, to lose lots of weight. Girls going through puberty are given a bit of extra fat to help their bodies prepare for womanhood. It's how God designed us, and it shouldn't be ridiculed or thought of as disgusting. Society needs to stop pressuring girls.

On another occasion, during the swimming carnival, I was due to participate in the fifty-metre breast-stroke race. At this point, I'd started growing some hair under my arms, but I didn't want to shave. I was still a child.

I put my arms up, readying myself to jump in, when all the kids started hassling me, laughing about my underarm hair. Some of the teachers laughed at me too. I got distracted, and when I did dive, I slipped on the water on the diving board, got my legs tangled in the metal poles that held it up, and hit my head on the edge of the pool. I finished the race, but no one helped me. I wasn't given an ice pack for my head and no one checked whether I was OK.

Last year during swim club, I realised this event had caused me to be afraid of diving into pools. I had gone years thinking I just couldn't dive properly. No, it was trauma and subconscious fear, not inability. I broke that fear by challenging myself to practice diving, first from the edge of the pool, then from the blocks. Within two weeks, I'd done it. Now I can dive from the blocks reasonably well and I'm no longer afraid.

As soon as I started growing body hair, I was hassled to get rid of it. When I was twelve, I had girlfriends repeating cultural lies to me, like, "You have to shave your underarms. You'll look ugly if you don't shave." "No boy will want you if you're hairy," and "It's wrong for girls to have hair." As if having body hair was a sin.

What is this big kerfuffle about girl's body hair? It's just hair. God gave it to us as a protective layer for our skin. We are meant to grow it. If females chose to shave, that's fine. I shave myself, now. But I shave because I choose to for my own reasons, not society's.

I have a real issue with people expecting pubescent girls and women to have hairless private parts. When we start growing into women, the natural process is to grow hair there. If you want a woman to be hairless there, that means you want them to look like a little girl there, which in turn means that on some level, you're attracted to little girls. And that is really concerning.

CHAPTER 4

A Trip to Tasmania and Another Move

In the spring we drove to Melbourne, then took the car ferry to Tasmania. Dad was worried the trip over would be really rough, seeing as it's a Bass Strait crossing. But the sea was still as a millpond.

We disembarked at Georgetown and drove south from there. We stayed a few days with our friends Raymond and Annette, on Hobart's Eastern shore.

On our first day in Tasmania, we went on a march through Hobart with Fusion. We held gold and green balloons and let them loose into the sky after the sermon. That march was filmed for the news.

Candace got a really bad case of gastro while we were in Hobart. She couldn't stop vomiting, so Dad had to take her to hospital. The nurses put her on a drip and Raymond and Dad prayed for her. We travelled to South Arm once she'd recovered, and stayed in a cabin near the beach. I started feeling sick while there. I really hoped I wouldn't get badly ill like Candace had.

We had a lovely trip around Tasmania, visiting Cradle Mountain, Rosebery and Cataract Gorge in Launceston. On our final night, we had dinner at a fancy restaurant and stayed in the upstairs apartments. We were due to catch the ferry the next morning.

I started feeling really ill during dinner. My stomach was so queasy, I couldn't finish my meal. I'd caught what Candace had earlier. Poor Breanna got a bad dose of it when we got home.

A New Rental

During the summer holidays of 1993, we moved to a little village in Many Waters County called Gulawayn; a lovely spot on Pleasant Estuary.

We lived in a cul-de-sac tucked underneath a pointy hill. A small creek flowed from the hills above, cascading down into our neighbour's garden. A tiny pocket of subtropical rainforest existed here, simply because of the little creek. Large man ferns straddled the creek on either side, and tall eucalyptus sprang up around it.

The creek flowed into Pleasant Estuary under a tiny railway bridge. During the dry, there wasn't much water in the creek. We'd have to walk down the little rocky track to see the waterfalls. Not so in the wet. Then, the water would jump happily over the small precipice in splashing torrents. There was so much water, we could see the falls from the road.

This little rainforest pocket was home to brush turkeys, satin bowerbirds and superb lyrebirds. A bird watcher's paradise. I already liked birds because Dad was a keen bird-watcher, but the satin bowerbirds gave me a real interest in bird watching. They were the prettiest birds I'd ever seen; with purple eyes and glossy, night-sky feathers shining in the sunlight.

We had some weird experiences in that house. We'd hear the alarm clock and try to turn it off, only to find it wasn't on. We'd go to answer the phone, only to find it wasn't ringing. Eventually, Mum worked out it was the lyrebirds. They were beautiful and they could mimic anything.

One afternoon while driving home from a family outing, we saw a male lyrebird displaying on a mound, right at the top of the falls. His tail was fully out and he was shaking it in order to attract the females. We were impressed, so I suppose the female lyrebirds were too.

Our neighbour had been a torch bearing runner in the Melbourne 1958 Olympics, he'd driven trucks, raced cars and served in a war. He told lots of amazing stories. The poor man had seen a lot though, and had become an alcoholic as a result.

One afternoon, I went over to ask him a question and he was in his car trying to kill himself. I ran to get Mum. We helped him back into his house, chatted to him and got him a cuppa and a snack. He recovered quite well, thank goodness!

For much of my life, I've wondered why I keep witnessing crises. Recently, I realised it's because of my gifting as a watchman and seer. God doesn't let me see bad things to hurt me; he does it because he trusts me to do something about it. God trusts his warrior princess. That's a great honour.

Our closest neighbour was a Christian woman, who became a good family friend. She'd prayed for good Christian neighbours before we came. We were an answer to her prayer.

Across the road from us in the cul-de-sac adjoining ours lived a friendly family. I made good friends with the eldest daughter, D'arna, at the primary school we both attended, and Candace made friends with Nicola, D'arna's little sister.

Up the road a bit lived a very community minded English couple. Their daughter also became a friend of mine during high school. They organised community parties twice a year; one for Christmas and one for the Queen's birthday. We had such fun at those parties! Bonfires and sparklers were lit, people talked, drank and were merry. An inevitable sing along would start later in the evening. Someone would begin and then everyone else would join in! It was a great neighbourhood.

When I was fifteen, I got a job as the community babysitter. The neighbours would ask me to mind their little ones so they could go on dates. I enjoyed it. It was good to know that the adults trusted me.

A New School

After the summer holidays, I started in year six at the local school. I became part of a small group of friends, including Beattie, Amira, D'arna, Annie, Cassandra, Amber and Liberty. Some of the things these girls did I didn't think were wise or good. I loved them, but I didn't like how they tried to convince me to swear, or how they sometimes held séances at lunchtime. Even though they said it was fun, I could tell those séances were having a bad effect on them. One lunchtime after they'd held one, Annie came back to our seat screaming and crying, saying the spirits told her she was going to die.

Something I really did like about my school friends, though, is that they all liked to sing. We had singing competitions during sleep overs and play dates.

I received lots of awards for my drawings. Liberty said I was really creative and encouraged me in visual arts and writing. She said that one day I would become a published author. Her encouragement helped me realise I was creative. As a result of her encouragement, I started contemplating a career in the arts.

A Challenging Birthday Party

In April that year, Annie had her birthday party. She told us she wanted to watch horror movies and hold séances. I asked my parents if I could go, and told them I wouldn't take part in the séance, but they said no.

Annie then changed her mind and said we wouldn't hold the séance. So I said I'd go. Mum and Dad were a lot happier about me going now that the séance wasn't going ahead.

But when I got there, she'd changed her mind about the séance again. I said, "Ok, but I I'm not doing it."

All my friends were really respectful of that. No one pushed me, which I was grateful for. While the others held the séance, I sat and talked with Cassandra, who didn't want to take part either.

Afterwards, we had a singing competition and watched movies.

Annie wanted to watch "It". I prayed I wouldn't get too scared. It was horrible. When we were going to bed, Amber was too frightened to go to the bathroom by herself. So I went with her and stood guard nearby. She kept saying, "Jules, are you there?" I kept reminding her that she was safe, I was happy that God used me to calm her down. In fact, Amber later said she always felt calm around me. I brought peace to those girls.

Next morning, we watched a cute movie called Ladybugs. I was just glad it wasn't horror.

My friends thought that horror movies were just entertainment and that séances were just a game, but I knew better. I had been taught that talking to spirits you don't know are good is not Godly, and I was also taught the dangers. Evil spirits can disguise themselves, so you could really be talking to an evil spirit when you thought it was your dead grandma.

ACT 2

Trauma Makes the Warrior Question Her Purpose

Dramatic music plays, rising to a suspenseful climax that leaves the warrior trembling, questioning her purpose, questioning herself...

CHAPTER 5

A Challenge to the Growing Warrior's Confidence

There was a spirit living on the property. It used to talk to me. I thought that because I hadn't summoned it, like you do in a séance, I should answer it, because it was polite to do so. I knew instinctively it was older than me and we are taught to honour and obey our elders. I thought I was doing the right thing. I thought it was my friend.

One day it said to me, "Do you need that Bible?" I hadn't read my Bible for a couple of days. I was struggling to get through something in the Old Testament. I replied, "No, you can have it if you want, I don't need it."

The next day, I couldn't find my Bible. I looked all over for it. I asked Mum if she'd seen it. She said, "Maybe the devil took it." Hmmm ...

I prayed that God would bring it back. The next day, it was back in the spot I always put it; on the desk beside my bed.

That spirit kept talking to me. One night it said to me, "Do you want Barry?" (Barry was a boy I liked.) I saw the spirit change its shape to pose as this boy. I said no and it went away. I instinctively knew it wanted something sexual from me, even though I didn't really understand sex yet.

I had a vision one night where I woke up and saw a set of playing cards on the ceiling. I didn't know what it meant but it scared me. I wonder now if God was using that to try and warn me that whatever spirit this was, it was a player and not trustworthy.

One afternoon, I came out of the shower wrapped in my towel, and went into my bedroom.

As I walked through the door, I heard a voice say, "Lie down and I'll press it." I looked around and couldn't see anyone. I figured it was the thing I'd been talking to. But its voice sounded different somehow; more menacing.

I lay down and I felt fingers touch my clitoris and start rubbing. Then I felt pain as the fingers moved up my vagina. I had an orgasm, which felt very scary and foul despite the bodily pleasure. I did not understand what had happened to me. Then I felt the spirit leave the room.

I stood up, wrapped my towel around me tighter and thought to myself, "That was wrong!" I had no intention of telling Mum and Dad. How would I have explained it?

During the weeks following, I felt scared, especially when I went to bed at night. I started behaving oddly, re-enacting the abuse in ways I could understand (something children do as a means of processing abuse) and thinking God wanted me to stay up all night to pray, sometimes while standing in weird positions in the corners of my room (such as on one leg).

Yes, sometimes God asks us to do strange things, but they always make sense within the context of the scriptures and the situation. Jesus would never say, "God will hate you if you don't get out of bed and pray for three hours." God loves us and never threatens us.

I was basically doing a strange form of penance; I believed this sin was my fault.

At one point the evil spirit even said to me, "It's your fault, because you're so disgusting. You made me want to do this to you!"

It's your fault evil spirit, not mine. I didn't even know what, "I'll press it" meant. I was looking around for a button.

You chose to hurt me. I didn't choose to let you. I was the victim. That evil spirit's sin did not change who I was, and it never could. I am still a good Christian girl, and I always will be.

A Triggered Warrior

I started high school in 1995 and made some great friends. I talked to some of my friends about God. I didn't deliberately set out to evangelise them, I have just always naturally talked about my faith. I remember that one boy asked me to explain how God could be real if he hadn't been created. I explained that God was always there; he wasn't made, he just was. I gave the analogy of God being like primary colours – you can't make them, they just exist, but all other colours come from them.

I'm still an evangelist.

In year seven, when I was turning thirteen, I developed the biggest crush I'd ever had on a boy named Jackson. The crush got a bit out of control, bordering on obsession. I asked him out on a date, and he refused in a really nasty way.

I went to talk to him about why he'd said no in such a mean way, and my hormones and all my hurts took over. I picked him up by the scruff of the neck and demanded he talk to me. I was so surprised. I have never done anything like that before or since. It was wrong. I'm sorry, Jackson.

Looking back, I can see that this was a trauma response.

Despite this patch of nasty behaviour, a lot of guys asked me out during high school; even from day one. Costa liked me on and off for our entire first year, and asked me out repeatedly. I wanted to say yes each time but I was too scared and didn't feel ready. Partly, it was because I felt too young. Partly it was because Mum and Dad preferred that I wait till I was sixteen, and I wanted to honour them. But mostly, it was because subconsciously, I was terrified of being assaulted again.

I carried around a cloak of fear wherever I went. I didn't fully realise I was doing this, and I couldn't get rid of it. Sometimes, when I felt threatened, I'd lash out and say things I later wished I hadn't.

Despite these difficulties, it was a good year. I made some good friends, found some great natural places, and worked out that I definitely wanted a career in visual arts.

CHAPTER 6

The Warrior's Identity Confused

Towards the end of year seven, one of the girls, Thelma, got it into her head to play some mean jokes on me, such as putting dead flies in my hair. She convinced Louise to do it too.

I'd tell them off repeatedly and eventually they'd stop whatever mean trick they were up to. Then they'd come up with a new nasty idea.

This continued all the next year until it got completely out of hand and became full blown bullying. They'd do things like take my pads out of my bag, colour them in red, and stick them onto the outside of my bag, or throw my lunch under buildings, or tell me to take my shoes off, then throw them into ants' nests.

The funny thing was; neither Thelma nor Louise behaved like that during school holidays. They were perfectly normal then. It was confusing.

A lot of the other kids in the class assumed I was, "letting them do it." That's a lie and a form of victim blaming. No one lets people treat them like that. The truth is, I often pulled them up on their behaviour. I'd say no, tell them they couldn't do it, tell them off if they did, tell my parents, get them to give me some of their lunch if they'd ruined mine, get them to give me more pads, etc. On a number of occasions, I threatened to tell the teachers if they didn't stop. They always said they would stop. And because they didn't engage in this kind of behaviour all the time, not even all the time at school, I'd give them another chance.

They ran out of chances eventually, because I got absolutely jack of it and took the situation to the year adviser. He asked me what punishment I thought they should have. I told him to tell their parents about their behaviour and give them after-school detentions.

The rest of that school year did not go well for me. I went from seat to seat, trying to settle somewhere. I became very argumentative at home, letting all my aggravation out where it was safe, and taking it out on Mum.

Boys continued to ask me out all through year eight, but I said no to each boy. I still liked Costa. I was angry with myself for not saying yes to him before, because I knew I hadn't dated him due to fear.

Instead of moving on, trying to go out with Costa became an obsession. Poor Costa. I practically worshipped him. No wonder he didn't want to talk to me much that year.

Not long after going to the year adviser about my friends' behaviour, I had a dream about Costa.

I was floating on a mattress in the air, above a small billabong surrounded by cliffs. I was hanging onto Costa's hand, trying to stop him from falling. He was saying, "Let go, let go!"

I didn't want to let go because I didn't want him to get hurt. I finally did let go, and he fell, but did not get hurt.

I knew upon awakening that I needed to let go of my desire to be with Costa. I needed to stop pursuing him. I told God I didn't want to like him anymore if God didn't want me to. I gave it up to God.

Upon return to school the next year, I didn't have those strong feelings for him anymore. I was so pleased. Costa said, "I knew you'd come to your senses!"

Not long after that, Thelma and Louise apologised to me. It was a good start to the year. We were proper friends for the remainder of high school.

Even during hard times, I always had my family and church family. Fun times with them allowed me to have something else to focus on. I began attending a Catholic youth group with Breanna. It was fun and I made new friends. We had Bible studies and meditations at our regular meetings, and on weekends, we hung out at parties and had dinner at each other's houses.

It was really nice to find somewhere I could be accepted for who I was, without feeling like I had to compromise myself in order to be accepted.

Church meetings were held at a house in Kookaburra's Rest, and we always felt the presence of God. There were several nature spots we frequented that always made me feel free of fear, anger and stress, too. One of these was Kookaburra's Rest Clifftop Walk. I liked the beautiful little beach in the small cove between Moody Bay and Kookaburra's Rest Beach. Sandstone made up the escarpment surrounding it, the clifftop bloomed with gazanias and freesias and pig face flowers opening to the sun, their green succulent tendrils cascading down the slope.

Our family often walked to this little beach, then stopped to admire the patterns in the sandstone, and watch the waves break on the outer rocky reef. One evening, after this walk, we stood on the cliffs back at Kookaburra's Rest and watched the sunset break over the Pacific Ocean. The colours changed from pink, to tomato red, to luminescent orange. Then the sun's golden rays slipped below the horizon, for a moment illuminating everything with gold, and the bright copper button of the sun sank into the velvet pocket of the sea and all was dark.

Family meant joy to the wounded warrior, and a safe space to continue being me.

Winter 1997 - First Overseas Holiday

In winter 1997, we went on a family holiday to the South Island of New Zealand. It was the first time us kids had flown in a plane. I remember looking out the windows at the mountains.

We landed at Christchurch and hired a campervan, then drove around the island for two weeks. At one park in Queenstown, it was so cold, Mum put on all the clothes she could fit into. She came to the door of the campervan looking like the Michelin Man! She had to come out sideways because she couldn't fit through. It was hilarious!

That afternoon, we took the chairlift to the top of The Remarkables and took in the beautiful view from the top. On the way back down, I saw a mountain goat. I thought, "Gosh, we are really up high if we are in the realm of the mountain goats!"

I shared a bed with Candace, because there weren't enough beds for us all in the van. She wriggled a lot! I couldn't sleep properly because she wriggled so much. She'd end up lying diagonally across the bed. I asked our parents if I could stop sharing with her, so they arranged for me to sleep in the bed above the driver's cabin. They asked Breanna to share with Candace for the rest of the trip. It was freezing up there, but I could layer up and at least not be disturbed by a wriggling sister.

We drove over Arthur's pass on the way to Mt Cook. It was beautiful looking out over the lake from the top of the pass. On the way up, Breanna remarked, "Dad, these mountains don't think about it do they? They just go up!" Dad chuckled in agreement.

We visited Franz Joseph and Fox Glaciers. At Franz Joseph, we walked across the rock scree and climbed partway up the glacier. There was a huge ice cave carved out beneath it, with a beautiful river running out from under it, created by ice melt. The colours were remarkable, blue, deep cyan, white, brown and yellow. The river had a really earthy smell, due to the minerals deposited into it from the glacier. I found the glaciers so fascinating.

Next, we took a trip to Milford Sound; a fiord in the south west of the country. On the trip down, we drove through a valley where loose rocks were perched on the surrounding mountains. There were signs everywhere saying, "Caution, frequent rock slides." Uh oh. When I saw those signs, I started praying we'd reach Milford Sound safely.

After getting safely through the valley, we had to drive through a tunnel. When I say tunnel, it was more like a hole through a cave, with a dirt road going through it. Mum gets claustrophobic, so she was saying, "I don't like this!"

Partway through the tunnel, we saw water pouring through a hole in the roof! Not just a trickle, a small waterfall! Dad was worried the water from the leak in the roof would freeze as it hit the road, creating black ice. He thought we'd go flying out the end of the tunnel like a bar of soap slipping out of a bathtub.

When we got to Milford Sound, we were so relieved to have arrived safely that we forgot to check the carpark for ice. We all got out of the campervan and promptly slipped over. Once we'd recovered, we went for a short walk to a nearby waterfall before having dinner at the pub.

After dinner, we decided to do some washing. We hand washed our clothes in the river flowing into the fjord, then hung them over the steering wheel, the bull bar, the chairs, and anywhere else we could find a free space. Then we went to bed. Next morning, we had steering wheel shaped undies, crumpled up frozen socks and bull bar shaped t-shirts. We still talk about that frozen washing.

Later that day, we went on a boat cruise to the ocean. We ferried past the waterfall we'd walked to the day before, and the captain nudged the nose of the boat underneath it. We sailed past a seal colony. It was enchanting watching them splash and play with each other.

After Milford Sound, we went on a paddle boat cruise across a lake to a farm. When we arrived, we were led to a paddock where highland cattle were kept. The farmer gave us a talk about them. He even let us milk one of the cows and stroke its nose, and Candace sat on it. We were served dinner in the farmhouse's formal dining room, which had high ceilings with beautiful engravings in the plasterwork. The waiter, who was dressed in a tuxedo, offered us drinks, while a lady played the piano. It was all very fancy.

Breanna was really excited because she'd been reading Jane Austen and she said she felt like she was inside the novel *Pride and Prejudice*. She was wearing her brown baby doll dress, and ever after, that dress was her "Lizzy" dress.

On the return journey, there was a sing along. Candace and I sat with the other guests around the piano and a musician led us in some old time sing along tunes.

On our next adventure, we crossed a lake at dusk. It was dark when we arrived at the jetty on the other side. We got into long tinnies, then sailed up the river flowing into the lake. We came to a cave. The tour guides tied all the boats together and we slowly entered it.

After a while, we stopped, and the tour guides turned off their torches. Suddenly, the cave was filled with a beautiful, otherworldly, blue glow. We looked up to the ceiling and saw that almost every inch of available space was taken up by glow-worms. They twinkled like stars in the sky. Glorious!

Everybody started talking in reverential whispers, so beautiful was the scene above us.

The tour guide explained how the glow-worms hunt, sending out strands of natural glue they excrete from their mouths. They let their gluey strands hang down and hope a meal in the shape of an insect will get trapped in them. Then they reel the strands back up with their mouths and eat their prey.

Our last stop was a cute little seaside town called Akaroa; built onto the side of deceased volcano. The crater had filled with sea water, making a delightful bay. On our first night there, we had dinner at a fancy restaurant overlooking the water. I remember the sticky date pudding and the lemon meringue pie – the best I've ever had.

On the way home from the airport, Breanna and I were talking about how funny it would be if people thought there was an official "Australian" language. I suggested they might think our place names were "Australian" words. Breanna laughed and then we made up a silly song. It went, "Banananananana mmbop diggy doo, Woy Woy, Wollongong, Woolloomooloo. Tangambalanga, Yackandandah, Gulawayn, Te-Anu." We sang it over and over, laughing. Admittedly, Te-Anu is a New Zealand place name, but it's the only name we could think of that rhymes with Woolloomooloo!

We had such great times on our family holidays! They are some of the best memories I have!

Interesting Times with God

For a season, as our house church stopped running, we didn't attend church at all. Then, out of the blue, Dad made friends with a local Anglican priest named Toni. She was great, really friendly and welcoming. She came over for meals and encouraged us to come back to church. Breanna and I started going to the youth Bible studies she held at her house.

Around this time, Dad made a drum. He said God told him to. We went on a walk in the bush up behind Hillside, looking for a hollow log. I was standing under a copse of trees when Dad yelled out, "I've got it!" I went over to him and he'd found a log about seventy centimetres long and completely hollow. He said, "This is the one."

We bought the log home, where Dad got to work chiselling out any loose or rotting bark from inside it. It took a long time. Then he sanded it down and varnished it.

Next, he bought a kangaroo skin from an Aboriginal fellow that lived nearby. He soaked that kangaroo skin in the bath for two days and nights. When it was soft enough, he stretched it over the wood and tied it tightly around the log. Behold, we had a drum!

When Dad went on prayer trips around Australia and New Zealand with his mates, he took his drum. It's been played all over the place, sounding out the rhythm of God's heart.

Dad has some great stories from his trips. One of my favourites is of two eagles tumbling together above a cliff. Dad said he and his mates had driven very early in the morning to a spot in the mountains. They were trying to pray but the flow wasn't happening. Then the two eagles appeared, falling from a great height together, tumbling, flapping, separating, and coming back together. Dad said it looked like they were dancing, like the eagles were transacting something for them in the spirit realm, and the men were then released to pray.

When Dad came home from his first New Zealand prayer trip, he told us he and his mates had been talking about exponential growth, and had been praying for finances to grow.

Not long after he returned, he and Mum went for a walk on Dolphin Sands Beach and a ten dollar note was washed up, just floating at the shoreline. He picked it up and brought it back home.

After that, Dad started finding money in other unusual places. He also saw gold dust fall from the air in a meeting, and once even semi-precious stones. God actually made it rain jewels! Amazingly, they didn't hurt anyone upon impact. That is miraculous in and of itself. Falling stones could cause a lot of damage.

CHAPTER 7

Some Horrors

A Near Drowning

When I was fourteen, after a family BBQ lunch, Mum, both of my aunts, Candace, Uncle Shark and I went for a swim in the pool.

After a while, Mum and the two aunts went back to the house, leaving me and Candace with Uncle Shark. A bit later, I popped upstairs for a snack. Mum suddenly asked me to go and check on Candace, which seemed odd, because Uncle Shark was with her. But I obeyed Mum and returned to the pool.

When I got there, Candace was floating face down in the pool and he was standing calmly next to her, not trying to help her at all. Then he repeatedly grabbed her neck, pulled her head up out of the water and plunged it back in, again and again.

When he looked at me, his face didn't look like the face I knew. His eyes had gone wild and dark and creepy; and a satisfied smile played on his lips.

I ran inside. "Mum, I think he's trying to drown Candace!"

Mum and I raced back down to the pool together.

When we got there, Candace was still floating face down in the pool, while he sat calmly on a deck chair with an evil sneer on his face.

Mum got in the pool and I stood on the step to hold Candace's unconscious body, while Mum worked out how to lift her to safety.

Once we had her out of the water, we laid her carefully onto the paving and gave her mouth-to-mouth resuscitation. She came to pretty quickly, thank goodness!

Mum asked my uncle, "What were you doing?"

He replied, "I'm not a very good swimmer and I thought I was going to drown, so I grabbed onto her."

That was his story. I know what I saw. The truth is he tried to drown her.

Once we'd got Candace into the house, my parents and I found a quiet spot in the garden to talk. Mum said she believed me. Dad was asking if she was sure and she said, "Yes, Jules doesn't lie!"

I could see Dad believed me too.

They were discussing what to do when Uncle Shark sidled up to us and deliberately put himself in the conversation. He talked Dad into believing him over me; convinced him it had all been an accident, and that I was just overreacting. So my parents, who ought to have rung the authorities, didn't.

Everyone there that day buried what happened deep down and trivialised it, buying his lies, because it was too scary to admit he was a murderer.

I was really brave that day. Not only by acting on my instincts and getting help for what I witnessed, nor simply by helping Mum save her, but also by sneaking into the house while no one was looking and attempting to call the ambulance.

The adults were not dealing with it properly, so I did, picking up the phone when no one else would. Unfortunately, Uncle Shark followed me inside and snatched the phone off me before I was connected to the ambulance. I was scared, so I didn't try again.

Even though I still have some trauma about not being listened to or taken seriously that day, it's time for me to face the fact that if it hadn't been for me, Candace would be dead. My bravery that day saved my little sister, and I am proud of that. It's time to lay the trauma aside and be thankful that God made me who I am: a brave, life-saving, warrior princess.

CHAPTER 8

A Boyfriend

My first real boyfriend relationship took place when I was sixteen. I thought at first that he was an answer to prayer. I felt like I was taking a step in the right direction to agree to be his girlfriend because it was a way of finally confronting my fear of relationships.

In the following pages are some reconstructed diary entries from that time.

1st week of November 1997, at school

My friend Maisy is friends with a boy called Samson. She knows him from being in school musicals.

He's friendly, but weird. I don't know if I like him or not, because he keeps staring at me. I mean creepy staring, not gazing at me adoringly like Costa used to.

He stands up on the balcony of E Block and watches me before coming to talk to Maisy. Like, creepy watching, as if he's planning something bad, not like watching me because he is too shy to come talk to me, but thinks I'm gorgeous. He's done this about three or four times.

I mean; maybe it is just that. Maybe he is just too shy to ask me out or something. But I don't like it. I wish he'd stop staring at me and watching me like that.

Then, when he talks to Maisy, he spends half his time sneaking stare sessions at me. It's really off-putting. I might have to tell him not to do it...

2nd week of November, at school
Samson's at it again! And these last few times he didn't even pretend to come down to talk to Maisy. He just stood there on the balcony, staring at me creepily. Stop it Samson!

March 1998, back at school
I'm in the musical! I'm a chorus dancer! Yay!
Samson came up to me after tryouts and asked if I was in the musical. He got all excited that I was in it and said he was in it too, as a main character. Well done!
He seems alright now. Maybe I shouldn't feel uneasy around him anymore.

March 20th
Samson and I have become friends. I've realised he is actually nice, and he's funny. We talk a lot now during practice. I like him now. I'm glad I'm not scared of him anymore.

March 31st
I'm starting to like Samson too, like, I have a bit of a crush on him. He's so funny and we get on really well. I wonder if we'll go out.

April 12th

We rehearsed the whole musical last night, and it was time to get changed and get ready to go home. I was heading up the stairs to the girl's change rooms when Samson came down the stairs. I said, "What are you doing? You aren't allowed in the girl's change rooms."

He said he hadn't been there, so I asked him why he was walking down the stairs then. His answer was that he had been talking to Nelly, which would still be inappropriate even if it is true, but I don't buy it. What was he really doing?

Then, when I began walking past him, up the stairs to go get changed, he began following me, then said he wasn't going to follow me; he just wanted to talk to me...

I mean, can't you talk to me in a more appropriate spot? And couldn't you wait till I was finished getting changed? Why follow me up the stairs?

Anyway, he began following me again, so I stopped on the stairs where I was, (third level up, only one to go), held up my hand to say stop, and told him, "You are not to follow me any further. If you want to talk to me, you can wait until I finish getting changed."

He agreed, and then I said, "And you're not allowed to sneak in and perv on me while I'm getting changed." I was really scared he would sneak in and look.

After I got changed, I went back down to where he was, and he grabbed hold of my hand and sort of led me to walk with him down the stairs. He kept on saying, "I'm not a perv, I'm not a perv. I hope you don't think I'm a perv."

I felt kind of numb, so I kept holding his hand and continued walking down the stairs with him.

When we got to the bottom, he guided me to sit on a big theatre block that is kept on the landing. We sat there cuddling, still holding hands.

It felt nice, and I put my head on his shoulder, and he snuggled into me.

Loretta found us there and asked if we were a couple. I said no, but he said yes. I'm confused.

April 16th

Well, that was the strangest conversation I've ever had!

We were on break from rehearsal, and I was standing with Ray, Samson, and a few others. Ray suddenly looked at me and said, "I'd really like to have a girlfriend."

Then Samson turned to me and said, "So would I!"

Then, under his breath, he said, "I want to rape someone."

I waited until the conversation was finished and most of the others had dispersed, then I confronted him.

Eventually he admitted saying it, but said he was only joking.

I said, "I'm glad you don't actually want to rape someone, but you shouldn't joke about it."

He looked away for a minute, looked back at me with this false guilty face, pouted at me and said, "I'm sorry. I won't say it again if it upsets you. I'll do that for you!"

Then stalked off in a huff.

He should know not to joke about rape. Why do I have to tell him these things? And he shouldn't have acted like he were doing me a favour by saying he wouldn't joke about it around me! He shouldn't joke about it at all!

May 12th

Mr Patrick told us that if we wanted to watch our favourite scenes, the ones that we weren't in ourselves, we could do so from backstage. So I watched Samson and Nelly do my favourite scene.

Then, when they came off stage, Samson looked at me really weirdly again. He looked me up and down and made this creepy turned-on noise in the back of his throat.

Nelly said, "Don't worry Jules, he's just eaten chocolate, and chocolate is an aphrodisiac", as if to excuse his behaviour.

He keeps on giving me compliments; I like that. But I didn't like the way he looked me up and down.

May 16th

Samson came over to me today while we were rehearsing for the musical in the hall, and asked me quite forcefully and pointedly, "Who do you like?"

I was too taken aback and embarrassed to tell him I liked him, so I said I liked Heath.

He asked why, and I replied, "Because he's cute and he's really good at art."

Then he asked, "What's he got that I don't? Why can't you like me?"

I looked over at him and he was looking at me with puppy dog eyes, like he was really sad.

I felt a bit bad that I'd made him so sad, so I asked if he was alright.

He said, "Yeah, I'm OK, I'm just a bit sad."

I asked what he was sad about and he said he was sad that I like Heath instead of him.

I told him that I did like him, I liked him too, and he looked up all excited, "Really?"

"Yes," I replied.

"What about Heath?"

"I like you more than Heath," I admitted.

"If I asked you out would you say yes?" He asked.

I said yes and he said, "Ok, I'll ask you out soon, in a couple of weeks."

"Why can't you just ask me out now?" I replied.

"I'm not ready yet." He said.

I asked him what he wasn't ready for and he said he just had to get a couple of things ready first. He wouldn't tell me what things.

I said OK and walked off mostly happy that I might finally have my first boyfriend, but also scratching my head at the, "I'm not ready yet", comment.

That was pretty weird!

May 30th

I asked God if I could go out with him and he said I could, but told me to be careful.

Ok, I will.

Yay!

When he asks me out I'm going to say yes.

CHAPTER 9

Red Flags

June 30th

He asked me out! I said yes! I'm really excited! I have a boyfriend!

He was acting weird though. Before he asked me, a group of us were walking back form the local theatre after seeing a play for drama. Suddenly, I became aware of his presence. I looked around and saw him and Ray power-walking towards us. Samson kept looking at me, and it was kind of scary how determined his walk was and how wide his eyes were. He looked like he was on some kind of war mission!

He came and asked me if he we could talk somewhere private.

He asked me out and I said yes.

But then he said something that seemed completely redundant. He said, "Ray likes you too, but I told him to let me go out with you, because I like you more!"

I mean, that's pretty weird isn't it? To bring Ray into it.

Then he asked me if I could go on a date with him the following weekend. I said no because I am going with my family on a holiday. He got upset, saying, "But we've only just started dating!"

He asked me to not go on the family holiday, but to stay home alone instead so he could come visit me. I said no again, told him I couldn't miss the family holiday because Dad had been planning it for weeks.

Ok, cool, we sorted that out. Excited for our date!

Saturday 31st June, 1998

We had our date!

It was fun, and I really like him, and I like how much he likes me, but he acted weird a few times. Is it normal to kiss someone without asking first?

While waiting for the train, he kissed me without asking, then grabbed me by the waist and pulled me onto his lap. He started kissing me again and I stopped him to ask; "Why are you making me sit on your knee?"

And he replied, "So I can kiss you better."

I mean, I like holding his hand, but couldn't he have asked me first before doing those things? Is that how it's really meant to go? I thought boys were supposed to ask first.

I don't know, because I've never had a boyfriend before.

I should ask Aleena. She'd know. She's had heaps of boyfriends.

When we got back to my place, my family were pottering around, doing housework, getting afternoon tea ready. Samson and I sat on the couch. We were alone in the lounge room, because everyone else was busy.

I felt really tired so I lay down on the couch. Not long after, he lay down next to me and started looking at me, checking *out my body really closely and inspecting my face, in detail. He was stroking my hair as he did this.*

I swear that's not normal! The way he was looking into my face, with his face all glowing; like he was worshipping me or something!

Dad came out and said, "Oi! Get off my daughter and sit up properly! We don't do that in this house!"

When he left, Dad warned me about him, saying, "I'm not anti-Samson or anything, but be careful of him. He was all over you."

That's three warnings now, so I'd better be careful. I'll pray for God to keep me safe.

I don't think he'd do anything to hurt me deliberately, but he is all over me, and too into me. It's weird!

July 9th

Samson and I had a lovely time at the foreshore walking under the trees, holding hands, and looking at the fish. It was very romantic. I've never felt this way about anyone before. He said I smelled good. I've gone all tingly!

The only thing is he told me off for telling a joke about the fishes going to school. I don't know why, he's always laughed at my jokes before.

I was brave and told him I didn't like him having me on a pedestal and I asked him to get me down. He said, "You're right. I have been doing that. I'll get you down if you don't like it." I had to tell him I'm not God and I don't like to be worshipped.

Why has he got me up there anyway? I'm just a girl.

July 10th

I told Samson today that I wanted to wait till marriage, which means I don't want to have sex. I feel better that I told him.

Now perhaps he'll respect me more.

July 12th

Samson made my skin crawl today...

I was in the library studying, when he came in to find me and sat opposite me at the table. We were just talking when he started looking me up and down again. Then he suddenly said, "Take your top off!"

I looked around; astonished and embarrassed, hoping no one else had heard him. I felt myself starting to go numb again, like part of me just shuts down when he talks like this, or when he does weird pervy things.

I'd looked away to gaze blankly out the window for a minute, and when I looked back at him, I said very quietly, "Not here."

I'm still not sure if I do want to do that, and we've only been dating for three weeks. And he should ask me first shouldn't he?

At the very least, he should not have said it like that, like I didn't have a choice in the matter. Gosh, I'm feeling incredulous at him now!

Incredulous. I like that word. We learned it in English.

It's a bit worrying that he wants to do that in public. What if one of the teachers saw us?

I'm starting to wonder if I should still be with him...

Saturday, July 14th

He came over today and wanted to talk to me outside, in private, out of earshot of Mum and Dad. He told me he'd cheated on me. He said he'd met a girl at the club and because he was drunk, he'd hooked up with her and kissed her. Then he realised what he was doing and walked away, and felt bad.

I was shocked, but I'm not that mad at him, because he looked really ashamed and crestfallen, like he was really sorry.

He was crying!

He said he still wants to be with me and he knows he did wrong and will I forgive him?

I am a little bit mad, because surely you could still have said no when you were drunk, Samson.

But I still love him, and he's still my sweetie. So I said I forgave him and gave him a hug, and he said thank you.

July 16th

At school the other day I asked if I could come over to meet his family. He said yes, acting happy that I wanted to meet them.

But when I asked him about it again today, he looked down at his shoes and declined.

And he's said no to me coming over to meet them a few times now.

Is he ashamed of me?

July 20th

Met his family. His Mum seems nice. So do his brothers and sister.

After talking to his family for a while, Samson wanted to go to his room.

Not long after being in there, he picked me up and threw me on his bed. I didn't know if I liked it or not. I mean, it was exciting, and you see that on romantic movies, so maybe it should have felt good.

But it made me cry, and I felt scared. I was crying and lying really still, like I couldn't believe what he'd just done. He lay down beside me and began kissing me and fondling my waist, hips, legs, then kissing my neck.

I did like that.

But I still feel alarmed. That's the word for it.

Saturday, July 21st

Today he stopped me in the middle of the road to kiss me. I couldn't believe it.

I said, "Not in the middle of the road, Sam!"

"Why not?"

"Because it's dangerous! What if we get run over?"

And he said, "It adds an element of danger."

I had to pull him off the road onto the path and stop him from grabbing my hand to take me back onto the road!

Doesn't he know that's dangerous? Is there something wrong with his head? I mean really, how stupid!

July 23rd

He rang me up and asked if I could stay the night at his house. I said no and he said, "Why not?"

I told him I didn't want to and he kept asking why, as if me not wanting to wasn't a good enough answer.

So I said, "Dad wouldn't want me to sleep over."

He wouldn't let it go, so I called out, "Dad, can I sleep over at Samson's house?"

Dad said no, he didn't want me to do that, and Samson finally gave up.

I finished that phone call feeling angry, with a bad taste in my mouth.

Why can't my "no" be good enough for you Samson?

July 24th

One of the teachers said something weird. He said, "Jules, I don't think you should go out with Samson. He doesn't treat you very well, does he?"

I looked at him blankly, said, "How do you know?"

He answered, "I heard him talking to his friends. He was saying not very nice things."

He wouldn't tell me what things.

Is Samson treating me badly?

Sometimes Samson is really nice. Sometimes he gives me really thoughtful gifts and tells me I'm so sexy. Sometimes he acts like I'm the only girl in the world. And sometimes he just acts like my old friend, telling jokes with me. A friend I can hold hands with and kiss.

I'm really confused.

Is Samson good to me or not?

July 25th

Samson has this weird thing about my body hair. If I've shaved very recently, he rubs his hand up my legs, acting all turned on by the hairlessness of them. But he stops at the knee. Whereas if I haven't shaved for a while, he'll do the same thing, but act angry about me not having shaved, then try to get higher up my leg with his hand.

One day at lunchtime, he even tried to slide his hand up to touch my vagina. At school! It's like he does it as a punishment for me not shaving as often as he wants me to.

I've started shaving more. Not every day, but four times a week instead of two. Maybe that will keep him happy, stop him from touching me.

July 27th

Samson rang me up and we were just chatting when his voice went all weird and mechanical and he said, "I want to get you into bed." It made my skin crawl.

"What did you say?" I asked.

He said, "I used the voice changer to say you're beautiful."

I know that's not what he said. Why are you lying to me Samson?

Why are you pressuring me, scaring me deliberately and being dishonest?

Just be normal for goodness' sake!

Saturday, July 29th

So I met up with Samson and Ray and we walked to the jetty. We sat there and chatted. Ray kept on looking over at me, them glancing at Samson, like he was worried about Samson being around me alone, like he was trying to protect me.

I wonder what that was about.

August 3rd

We were chatting at a party when he asked me if there was anything particular I wanted to talk about. I wanted to talk about God, so we discussed my faith and why he doesn't believe for a while. Then he said it was his turn and he wanted *to talk about sex. He looked at me and said, "Oh, sinful," in mock pious Catholic tone. Then, "You're not like that are you?"*

I answered, "No, it's a part of life."

I thought it was a good thing that he wanted to talk about sex, because I thought maybe he was going to clarify the boundaries in our relationship.

But what he said shocked me.

He asked, "Do you masturbate?"

I stared at him blankly for a couple of seconds because I was so shocked, then I answered, "I've tried it once."

He asked, "Where you just experimenting or were you feeling a bit hot?"

I didn't like the way he said hot, like it really excited him, with his eyes going huge again, and all sparkly.

I answered, "I just wanted to see what it was about."

I paused, then asked him, "Do you?"

*He said, "Yes, I look at porn. I look at the girls while I'm masturbating. I wish **you** were in there, one of the girls in it!"*

I felt sick.

Then he tried to explain a bit about the type of porn he looked at, said it was called gonzo or something, started telling me details, but I just shut down. My mind went somewhere else. I didn't want to hear it.

I have a vague feeling of alarm, that something about what he looks at is violent, but I don't remember exactly what. I have this vague sense that I'm in danger, but once again. It's really dull, like I can't hear the siren going off or something, if one even is going off.

Is there a siren sounding?

Or is everything OK?

Is it normal for boys to talk like that?

I feel scared.

Arabella told me, "Samson loves you, you know. You've got him wrapped around your little finger. He'd do anything for you!"

I sat pondering this for a while, thinking, "That's not right! I don't want to have him around my finger. I want us to be equals."

Now I'm wondering if perhaps I'm too demanding of him. He seems to get mad at me a fair bit for little things. Like when he bought me an artwork, and I didn't immediately know where to put it, and he seemed really mad that I hadn't put it on the wall straight away. I ended up taking my birthday cards down early so I could put the picture up, to please him, so he wouldn't be upset about it anymore.

And he's complained about me not paying for our dates, about him "having" to pay for me, even though he's the one who offers to pay. I guess I could pay for some dates.

Maybe I am a bit selfish. I'll try to be nicer. I don't like him being mad at me.

August 9th

Ray keeps on turning up on our dates.

I wonder what he's doing. It's like he's trying to keep an eye on me or something. That's three times now.

August 12th

We were walking through the playground at school, when Samson suddenly turned to me and asked if I'd have a golden shower with him.

I had no idea what he was talking about, so I said, "What's a golden shower?"

He said, "It's where you urinate on your partner."
Ew!
I said no, incredulously, and he said, "Why not?"
"Because it's disgusting!"
"No, it's not! Why do you think that?"
"Because it's a waste product!"
I mean, why does he have to be told this stuff?
Just as he was telling me that he'd been talking to that girl on the internet, the one he's been chatting to for a while, Mrs Lovett walked past.
Then, after I'd told him not to talk to me about it anymore, Mrs Lovett turned to us and said, "Ain't love grand?"
I thought to myself, "This isn't love."

August 16th
Yesterday, he rang me and asked me if I'd touch his penis.
Ew!
I told him no and he kept asking and asking, over and over, until I said yes just to shut him up!
I was really scared! I just wanted the phone call to end.
Mum suggested that I tell him not to speak to me like that and tell him I'd break up with him if he ever does it again, then watch his behaviour, and break up with him if he doesn't stick to my boundaries. I thought that was a good idea, so that's what I did today at school.
I confronted him and told him that I didn't want him to talk to me like that. He asked if that's why I'd hung up on him.
I said yes and he said he was sorry that he'd scared me.
I was thankful for that.

Then I told him never to speak to me like that again and that if he ever did, I'd break up with him. I told him he had to treat me better if he wanted me.

He said sorry and agreed to be good, so I accepted his apology, and we are still going out.

Monday 19th August, Spring Holidays

Am I supposed to show him my breasts? Is that what girl-friends have to do? Was I wrong to not want it like this?

I was lying on my bed and he was sitting beside me on a chair. He suddenly reached over, pulled my top up and started trying to fondle my breasts. Then he said, "And the bra covers the whole breast. Oh well, I'll just play with what I have."

I looked at him and said, "You can take it off it you want."

But I didn't really mean it. I only said that because I felt confused. Him touching my bra made me feel excited, but I hadn't actually wanted him to touch me before that, hadn't even been thinking about it.

And he didn't ask! He keeps just doing things without asking.

Anyway, just as he was trying to figure out how to get my bra off, Mum and Dad came home, so he stopped. Phew! Saved!

He asked me if I'd do that with him at his house and I said yes, partly because I was kind of getting aroused, even though I didn't really like it, but also to please him, because it seems like he isn't going to let me say no for much longer.

When we walked down to the jetty later, he started touching me again. At the jetty! Then he tried to convince me to let him touch my breasts at his house.

What is his problem?!

Also, now that I think about it, that thing with following me up the stairs to the girls' change rooms; Loretta told me he followed her and did actually perv on her! Then she warned me about him, saying, "Don't go out with him, he's a leech!"

Oh, I'd forgotten that! Oh! Maybe I should actually break up with him...

CHAPTER 10

A Nightmare

August 26th, at his house

He rang me this morning, asking if I could come over. I asked if his parents were home, and he said they were.

Just before I left to walk to his house, Dad said, "I don't think you should go today, Jules. I've got a bad feeling about you going to his house today."

I said I was going, and Dad said, "Ok, but just be careful."

When I got there, Samson came to the door in his pyjamas. I felt really alarmed, I had a real sense of foreboding.

I asked him whether his parents were home, and he said his mum had gone to work. The foreboding increased. Had he been lying to me?

He grabbed my hands and said, "Come to bed," in a low growl.

I was really alarmed now, but my feet just followed his, like they had a mind of their own.

When we were beside his bed, we started kissing, which I was enjoying, but then he picked me up and threw me on his bed again, jumped on top of me, pinned me down, took my top and bra off without asking and started touching my boobs!

I was really scared. I just sort of froze ... but then I kissed him back.

I realised what was happening was dangerous, and that kissing him back was a mistake, so I rolled away from him, hoping that was enough to get him to stop, but he followed me to the other side of the bed.

I was feeling really scared, and shocked, and was just starting to process what he'd done, when he got this really intense, excited look on his face. His eyes went dark, and he looked at me like he was a lion and I was his prey.

He grabbed my throat in both hands and strangled me. I was looking into his eyes. He was enjoying it. He was turned on by hurting me.

I was so scared, I blacked out. I came to I don't know how long later, and he was lying on top of me, with this sick satisfied smile on his face, staring right into my face again.

I asked him croakily, "What just happened?" And he said, "Oh it's alright, I just strangled you. Don't worry, it was fun."

Finally, he got up off the bed and went to the toilet. I was free.

I started crying. Deep sobs all choked up that couldn't fully escape because I was too scared to let him hear me cry.

I put my clothes back on. It was hard. My fingers wouldn't seem to work. I collapsed on the floor at the foot of his bed, sobbing uncontrollably and shaking, rocking myself back and forwards with my hands above my head, cowering.

He came back in and saw me, said, "What's wrong?"

I sobbed at him, barely able to look up. "You didn't ask me! You didn't ask me to do those things! You didn't!" I yelled.

I started rocking myself faster.

He said, "What do you mean?"

I answered, "You didn't ask me if you could touch my breasts! You didn't ask!"

He looked at me calmly and said, "You know you can tell me if you don't want to do something. It has to be consensual."

I asked him what that meant, and he said, "You have to say yes." And he looked at me like he meant he wasn't going to give me a chance to say no.

Then he asked if I wanted to do something else for a while. I said yes, so he pulled a book from his bookshelf, and we read to each other for a while.

I felt relieved. "He's stopped. I'm safe now. He's gone back to his sweet self", I thought.

But I was wrong. He was never sweet. He was a predator and I was his prey...

He asked if I wanted to go home. I did want to, desperately. I really wanted Mum and Dad, I wanted to feel safe again. I was about to say yes when I had a vision. I saw myself walk to the train station to catch a train home. But he followed me to the train station, snuck up on me, strangled me to death and left my body at the station. I knew from that vision that it would be more dangerous to leave than to stay, so I stayed.

I suddenly felt really tired, so I asked if I could lie on his bed. He said yes, so I walked over to it and curled up there, closed my eyes. But he followed me and started with the assault all over again.

He touched me for about half an hour, then asked, "Do you want to have a shower?"

I was thinking, "Why does he want me to have a shower? Do I smell?"

Then he said, "Do you want to have a shower with me naked?"

His eyes had gone all predatory again; that same dazzling, intense blue-eyed gaze, all sickly excited.

I said, "No!"

But he wouldn't take no for an answer. He wore me down until I agreed that I would have a shower with him, topless, but not naked. I was not taking my bottoms off for anyone.

"Well, you have no spare clothes, and if you have a shower in your clothes, you'll have nothing dry to wear home. So you may as well just have a shower with me naked."

I said no, I wasn't going to get naked for him. He pleaded again and I said, "Find me some board shorts then. No board shorts, no shower."

That made him stop pleading and actually find me some shorts. I told him I didn't want to get changed where he could see me, so he led me into his mother's room, so I could change there.

I'd just stripped naked and was about to put the shorts on when I turned around and saw him, leaning against the door frame, watching me. He said he wouldn't look, and there he was, looking.

He looked my naked body up and down and made that same disgusting low growl in the back of his throat.

I shook my head, smiled at him, (I was too scared not to), told him to go away and let me finish getting changed.

He left the room but the damage was done. I felt really unsafe now.

I came out, ready for the shower, and said, "Actually, I do want to go home."

He gave me a serious, evil look and said in a much lower voice than normal, "It's too late now. You've had your chance."

Then he locked all the doors and windows. I was trapped.

He made me have that shower. I stood there in the water, wishing it was over, wishing I could get free, with him pawing over my breasts again. It was horrible!

Finally, I heard a car drive up. His family were home. I'd been saved.

So I thought ...

He got out of the shower, barked at me to hurry up and get dressed, then danced around the living room singing, "We got away with it, we got away with it!"

No, you got away with it!

When his family finally came inside, Samson was standing by the window, looking out, acting "normal."

I came out and sat on the lounge, tried smiling, tried talking to his family. We had a good chat and at last I felt safe again.

We hadn't been sitting there very long when Samson motioned for me to follow him. He led me into his little sister's room, said, "Sshh," then got me to lay on her bed.

I thought it was pretty weird that he wanted to be in his sister's room.

I told him to keep the door open, which he did, then he lay next to me and started kissing and cuddling me, saying he loved me and that I was beautiful. I felt loved by him for the first time that day, so I stayed in his arms.

Then suddenly, he got up off the bed, shut the door and got that intense look again. I knew I was in real danger! I knew he was going to do something bad. I wanted to get up and leave, but I was frozen.

I watched him come to the bed, watched him lie next to me, felt him kissing my neck, heard his breath get shallower.

Then he suddenly stuck his hands down my undies, without asking, and started rubbing my clitoris.

I felt myself go all stiff, like a board.

I slapped his hands away three times, but he didn't listen. Instead, he grabbed my hands, pushed them away, and kept touching me. I thought, "He's not listening. I'll just have to go with it."

Even though I didn't like it, even though I was scared, I felt my body start to respond. He kept on rubbing and rubbing, and then he rubbed my vagina and stuck his fingers up there. It didn't hurt this time, but I didn't like it. Didn't want it. I'd told him early on that I didn't want to do this. He was breaking all my boundaries.

Eventually, I yelled at him to stop in a really commanding voice and he looked at me in surprise and stopped abruptly. Phew! Thank you God!

Then he came and cuddled me, said he loved me over and over.

I had to pretend everything was normal, but everything was not. What the hell just happened? I don't know but I didn't like it and now I'm really scared of Samson. Like, terrified!

CHAPTER 11

The Nightmare is Buried

Saturday 2nd September, first weekend since being back at school

Samson came over and apologised to me for something, not really sure what he was saying, but I felt really scared and I wanted to get out of there. I don't feel safe around him anymore. He didn't seem genuine either, because there was no sorry in his eyes, and he wouldn't look at me.

I wasn't really listening. I went blank and shut his voice out, stared into the distance.

What was he apologising for?

September 10th

Haven't heard from Samson in over a week. What is going on?

Saturday 17th September

Wrote Samson a letter, asking if he's trying to break up with me. He said yes, he didn't love me anymore.

Told my friends and burst into tears. I feel shattered.

September 30th

He was cheating on me. The whole time we were in a relationship. I keep trying to confront him but he just walks away and ignores me. He refuses to give me a reason for cheating, and he won't answer the phone.

I realise now he was dishonest with me the whole time. Even to his friends! He played the part of the devoted boyfriend while playing around. I am so upset I am getting really bad headaches, and I can't concentrate on my schoolwork.

I don't get headaches.

My friends are really worried about me. Something is really wrong, but I can't seem to remember exactly what.

October 1st

Loretta asked me a really weird question. She said, "Did Samson give you a hickey?"

I said no.

She said, "Why do you have those bruises on your neck then?"

Bruises? What bruises?!

Thursday 3rd October

Ray came looking for me and asked, "Did he rape you?"

I said he tried to but I was too strong for him. Ray asked what I meant and I said quietly that he convinced me to do some things I didn't want to do. Then he said, "But he wouldn't..." implying that Samson wouldn't have physically forced me.

I said no to help him not freak out, but I think I was lying.

I can't quite remember now what exactly he did that was forceful. I know I could look through this diary, read what I've already written, but I can't seem to get myself to. Every time I try to read it I get the shakes!

I'm not really sure what happened to me now. Everything is so messed up in my head.

I do know I didn't want to do a lot of what he wanted to do that day. Was it rape? Is that why I'm so scared?

My friends took me aside and asked if he hurt me. I burst into tears and they said, "It's just, you made it sound like he raped you."

I said his penis did not go into my vagina. I mean, that means it isn't rape, doesn't it?

They then said he shouldn't have made me do anything I didn't want to do. They asked if I'd told my parents. I said I couldn't because they want me to wait till marriage. Now I've disobeyed them haven't I? I feel so ashamed, wretched!

They told me I should at least tell a teacher, so I had a think about which one I can tell.

Friday 4th October, just after school

*I finally got the courage up to go and tell Mrs Tucker what happened with Samson. I was on my way to her office, climbing up the stairs, when **he** appeared with Ray! I froze.*

He looked at me, and in in that look I saw a threat, saw that somehow he knew I was going to tell a teacher what he'd done, what I can remember anyway, and that if he found out about me telling, he'd kill me.

I was so scared, I ran all the way to the other side of the school!

I have decided not to tell anyone what he really did. Because I don't want to be dead!

October 18th

A couple weeks later and I've calmed down, have almost forgotten how bad he was to me. I finally got to talk to him about why he cheated, and all he said, (well mumbled while looking at the ground), was, "Well you didn't give me what I wanted, so ..." And walked away!

Is it my fault he left me for someone else? Should I have been different? Should I have given him sex?

But I really didn't want to and I think he should have been OK with that.

October 19th

I told Mum he cheated on me, and she asked if I'd slept with him. I said no. But did I? There's a rumour going around the school that I'm a slut and that I lost my virginity to him. I'm still a virgin because his penis did not enter my vagina. But I did other things with him, so am I a slut, like they say?

I feel really guilty, confused and ashamed...

November 9th

I got on the wrong bus! I don't know how I did that!

I had been talking to Samson's brother, Jolly, when Jolly started going through my bag without asking, grabbed my contraceptive pills out of one of the pockets and started waving them around, demanding I tell him why I had them. I calmly told him I was staying at Kalina's house and I had to take them each night to help with my irregular periods.

He didn't believe me! Instead, he started accusing me of being a slut! But it's true about my pills! The doctor prescribed them to me because I kept bleeding and my periods were all over the place! I didn't make it up! Why doesn't he believe me?

Then he said something about Samson and I just blacked out, stopped hearing him. I was so scared, I jumped on the first bus I saw without looking at where it was going, and just mindlessly assuming it was my bus. And halfway to Hillside, I realised where I was, came to from my trance like state and saw I was on the wrong bus! I had to get off and find my way home from there!

Oh my goodness. I must have been so frightened about what Jolly was saying I went somewhere else in my head.

November 10th
We had to watch the year twelve drama performances today. Samson was performing.

I felt so scared and apprehensive about it. I really didn't want to go!

The teacher said I had to watch it so I gritted my teeth, walked in, and took a seat. I was sort of OK when it was the other year twelves performing. I was managing to hold it together. But I was getting more and more nervous as it got closer to his turn.

Then, when he came on, I just shut down, couldn't handle it.

I curled myself up into a ball and didn't watch, began rocking myself backwards and forwards, just hoping he'd hurry up and finish.

When he was done, I ran out of the room to get my breath back. I hadn't even realised I'd been holding it.

Our drama teacher took me aside afterwards and asked me if Samson had hurt me. I said no because I can't tell her. I can't tell anyone.

But I wanted to say yes and I don't think she believed my no.

She asked, "Are you sure?" She even asked if he'd beaten me or anything. I said no. But did he?

I know he did something really violent, but I can't remember exactly what now, my brain's already shutting it all out.

November 14th

I can't go into Coles, where he works, by myself. I start shaking. I make myself go in when I'm with family, but I always feel my legs trying to run away.

I've been acting really weird around boys too. At Venturers, I screamed when Billy touched my arm.

I can't stand to be hugged by boys who aren't my Dad or Grandpa anymore, and I keep jumping back from boys I don't know well. What is going on? Why am I doing this?

I hope I get back to my normal, happy, bubbly Jules again, soon!

CHAPTER 12

Life After Abuse

Not everything that happened that year was bad. I have several very good memories too. If I look at that year as a whole, I can see there are a lot more good memories than bad. It's as important to celebrate the good times as it is to lament the bad. I am determined to find the joy.

My first good memory from that year is of being chosen as a peer support leader, something I had really wanted to do. I was really excited to help the younger students.

I remember being in the musical. It was really rewarding and enjoyable learning all the songs and dances, and it was thrilling being on stage. I made good friends with two other girls who were also in the musical, who both had the same quirky sense of humour as me.

I loved drama classes. I enjoyed performing our own original plays and learning clowning skills and mime. Our drama teacher was very eccentric and jolly. She had the biggest laugh.

I enjoyed careers classes. We explored future job options. I already knew I wanted a career in the arts so it was a matter of working out exactly what. I looked at signwriting, screen printing, modelling, graphic art and lithography. For work experience, I was placed in the graphic design office at a local newspaper.

The peer support camp was awesome. The year tens and sevens came together, each of the year ten support leaders leading their groups of year sevens in activities, and teaching them about friendships and negotiation skills. We went kayaking, swimming, walking and dirt bike riding. We did archery and ropes courses, and we took turns on the flying fox.

I remember getting a great mark for my major art piece, and it being displayed at the school awards night.

The year ten formal was really fun. We had a buffet dinner at a local restaurant, then we had a disco. My friend hired a limousine to take some of us back to the after party. It was really special!

Later, I expressed my faith in another major school art piece: a series of three paintings featuring animals that were in the process of overcoming the surrounding chaos. One piece had a butterfly flying out of a vortex filled with burning space junk. One had eagles soaring towards heaven. And one had a frog jumping up to the blood of Jesus in order to escape falling into a chasm. This was my symbolism for the transformative love of Christ, how he saves us from the chaos that comes against us in this fallen world. And subconsciously, it was my declaration of freedom. Making art about overcoming hardship was a subconscious decision to help me deal with my trauma.

Another way I began overcoming my trauma was through close friendships. Me and my friends spent many a summer afternoon; playing in the pool, watching movies, and walking to the nearby waterfall. I liked sitting at the bottom of the falls, watching the bees buzz around the wild chamomile that grew there, admiring the thin veil of water as it tumbled over the rocky ledge.

In autumn that year I joined the local Venturers group. We went kayaking, night fishing and camping. We cooked shared meals. We wore our full uniforms and took part in the ANZAC service one year. We did overnight hikes and took part in competitions. We painted a mural on the wall of the Scout Hall and learned how to use a two-way radio.

Bronte and I became friends and used to regularly walk down to Gulawayn jetty to go swimming. It was in a little park behind the highway; a beautiful spot with a grassy picnic area, a playground, a change room and a little beach. We would jump off the jetty into Pleasant Estuary, swim around, then sunbathe on the jetty. One warm summer day, we walked down together as usual. We were about to jump in when we saw a stingray. Even after it swam away, we were too scared to jump in. We finally faced our fear when two of the local boys jumped in, and we decided we didn't want to be outdone.

The water was always warm there, and at night it was often filled with bioluminescence. It was beautiful sitting on the jetty under the stars, watching the water glow.

I remember the first time I saw the glow in the water. I put my hand in and scooped up tiny glowing particles. Now my hand looked like it was covered in tiny jewels. We had a great time that night, playing in the bioluminescence.

Another time, I saw the bioluminescence during one of Bronte's parties. A group of us were sitting together on the jetty. I pointed out the flashes in the waves. The others were too high to notice. I hadn't smoked anything so I watched the bioluminescence instead. I swear I had more fun playing in the natural glow than they did getting stoned.

I remember hiking through the bush to a Scout camp in Hillside. I loved the beautiful section above an escarpment overlooking a deep valley, across to the opposite cliffs. I liked singing there because the natural acoustics made beautiful echoes.

On another hike, we started at Hillside and walked to Dolphin Sands, stopping to camp the night at Hillside Brook, one of my favourite spots in the world. A beautiful waterfall cascades over tall rock walls, then leaps over a large boulder to land in a pool of crystal turquoise water surrounded by rainforest. After setting up camp, we all had a swim in the natural pool, then climbed up some rocks to stand right under the waterfall. That night, while the others were drifting off, I had another swim under the stars.

At the end of 1999, we attended a combined Scouts team challenge event.

All the Scout groups from the surrounding areas met up in a nearby valley. Each team had to hike for three days, stopping each night at a different spot along the way. We had to do different activities along the way too, such as orienteering, ropes courses and craft challenges.

Each night, after setting up camp, we had a shared dinner in the mess tent, then danced till we dropped in the rec tent.

A Small Amount of Faith in the Opposite Sex is Restored

On one of the Venturer's camps, Fin was flirting with me. At one point I was taking a shower and I heard him call out, "Hi Jules."

I called back, "You're not looking through the window, are you?"

He said, "No, I'm just hanging out some washing."

(There was a line behind the shower block).

Phew. I was so relieved. I was glad to know he wasn't a perv, like Samson.

Another time, a boy called Jamie asked me on a date. I didn't like him like that, so I declined and was very refreshed when he didn't try to convince me to say yes. The respect he showed me allowed me to begin to see that not all boys were bad.

My faith in men began to be restored because of the behaviour of people like Fin and Jamie.

CHAPTER 13

Our Own Home

During this time, we moved to a house in Woodsville, backing onto a local creek. We had a bright, airy lounge room that Mum painted blue and yellow. I painted a mural on my bedroom ceiling.

The property had a large backyard, and there was a huge gum tree right in front of the house. The bell birds roosted in it, and one day I even saw one up close. Many birds visited our garden, and one morning, I awoke at dawn and counted all the different bird calls; twenty-one of them. I was really excited to tell Dad when I got up.

Nearby was a beautiful walking track that climbed up a steep hill, past a craggy escarpment surrounded by trees, onto a rocky plateau. I used to sit there and look out over the valley. Further up the track was a waterfall flowing from some old railway dams. I used to stand at the top and watch the water whoosh down to the valley below.

Next to our house was a small pocket of bamboo forest, backing onto the creek. One afternoon, Candace decided to go exploring in the bamboo without telling us. Mum and Dad were looking for her, calling out to her, but they couldn't find her. Dad was beginning to think the worst, wondering if someone had taken her.

I knew in my spirit that she was in the bamboo, so I told Mum and Dad that it was alright, I believed God was keeping her safe. I offered to go find her.

I walked into the bamboo forest, calling Candace's name.

When I found her, she was watching the birds in the creek. I asked her what she was doing, and she said she'd just wanted to explore.

I took her back home and Mum and Dad were so relieved!

One morning, God woke Mum up with a vision, and she knew someone had to proclaim it. When Dad and his mates wouldn't do it, she realised God wanted her to paint it.

She was scared. All her life she'd been told she couldn't paint. People discouraged her, they said her work didn't look real enough. She still wanted to learn to paint despite the discouragement she'd experienced, so she was really excited to start high school art classes. Unfortunately, her teacher didn't know how to paint. She only taught her students art history. Mum was so disappointed. She stopped painting after that. That is, until God told her to start again...

So after Mum's revelation that *she* was to proclaim the prophetic word within her dream through a painting, she got started. She painted a bush scene with crows flying east from the tops of the gum trees, the flock led by one crow with his wings turning gold. Their movement depicted the winds of change.

In April 1998, Dad went on long service leave from his job. He went on lots of bushwalks with Mum during this time, and spent more time with us kids. When he went back to work three months later, his boss said, "What are you doing here?" He replied, "I've come back to work. I've finished long service leave."

He was told they had no more work for him; that they'd forgotten about him. When he complained, he was sent to do some vey menial tasks, instead of being given back his old responsibilities.

A few weeks later, they retrenched him.

Dad spent two years looking for work. He tried really hard. But he couldn't find anything suitable.

During this time, Dad bought a boat from the local marina. Mum and Dad painted her yellow and white and we named her Sea Sparkle. We went all over the coast in her, on family adventures. We sailed over to Washy Bay, where Dad taught Breanna and me how to drive the boat. We would sail under White Bridge to Reedy Flat, and we travelled through the narrow mouth of Pleasant Estuary out to Ribbed Bay, past Dolphin Sands and around Rocky Island. The swell could get rough out there.

Some of my favourite memories from being on the boat are when we sailed into Annie Bay and I kayaked to the waterfall, and when we sailed all the way to Agnes Bay, part way up the Agnes River. On the way home, we saw a group of juvenile sea eagles taking turns to dive into the water and catch fish. An amazing sight!

Dad developed a bad case of anxiety bordering on OCD, due to the stress he was under trying to find a job. He kept getting knock back after knock back. He decided to retrain as a librarian. I remember him writing essays late into the night as he worked to complete his degree. The stress of it all got to him and manifested as extreme anxiety.

He couldn't just leave the house, lock the door and go out anymore. Now he had to check the door several times before leaving. This behaviour manifested the most after being out on the boat.

We'd finish our boating trip for the day, row back to shore and put the rowboat back in its spot, and that's when Dad would say, "Did I lock the boat?"

I'd reply, "Yes Dad."

He'd ask again. I'd assert that he had. Then he'd start on a spiral of self-doubt, ask a few more times, and finally say, "I'm just going to check."

He'd untie the rowboat, set it into the water and row back to check the locks on Sea Sparkle.

Once he was back ashore, he'd again ask me if he'd locked the boat. I'd tell him he'd just rowed back to check, but that didn't stop his doubt, so he'd go back to check once again.

After a few months of this, it got so bad, he'd go back to check five times. Finally, I worked out that if I went with him in the rowboat to watch him check the locks, I could say, "I saw you check, Dad. She's locked."

That helped.

It took a while for him to get used to this routine, and at the start, he'd triple check the locks. But with time, this lessened, until checking twice with me watching was enough.

I was so relieved! I was tired of having to wait for him, freezing on shore.

Breanna Moves Out

At the beginning of 1998, Breanna moved to North Tower to study at university.

At first, she lived in a flat with her friends, Johanna and Bob. It was not a nice flat. The stairs up to the bedrooms were steep and uneven and it was old and run down.

We used to have parties at that flat. Johanna would hang the inner bag of a cask of wine on the washing line. Then she'd get us all to stand around it while she spun it round. Whoever the goon bag stopped in front of had to take a swig. She called it, "Goon of Fortune!"

When Johanna was really drunk, she used to cook lots of pasta. She'd say, "Everyone's hungry now," and put the pasta on to boil. Then she'd say, "We need to test if it's ready."

Instead of just taking a forkful of pasta and tasting some, she'd say "I'll throw some up to the ceiling. If it sticks, it's ready."

But she never just took a small amount. No. She'd take the whole colander full and toss the entire lot up into the air. Quite a bit would stick to the ceiling and whatever didn't stick rained down on us in a shower. Ah Johanna, there's no one like you.

Breanna begun dating a school friend soon after and she moved in with him and some other friends. At this time, she started taking drugs. She said she had it under control, but she became more and more unhealthy. I didn't know how to tell her she needed to stop. How do you tell your older sister that what's she's doing isn't good for her health?

I wasn't sold on her relationship with Gus either. None of us were. He was a nice enough man, but he had severe depression, and he wouldn't go out with Breanna on dates. He just wanted to hang around at home all the time. I realise the depression wasn't his fault, but it wasn't good for Breanna. She kept trying to fix him and it took a toll on her.

She finally broke up with him six years later. It just wasn't working. It was hard to tell her I was happy about it, but I was. She'd got sucked into the Gus black hole and finally got out. We had our old, happy, chirpy Breanna back. Hooray!

CHAPTER 14

Church and Family Adventures

At the beginning of 1999, a new girl called Clarissa joined most of my classes. She was really pretty and confident and I found out a bit later she was also a Christian. She was really open about her faith. I hadn't been open about mine for a few years, apart from with Samson. I told Clarissa one art class that I was a Christian too. She asked me what church I went to. I said I didn't go to church, so she invited me to come along to hers. Her openness inspired me to start talking about my faith again. I'm not sure what scared me off talking about it in the first place.

Not long after that, Clarissa invited me to attend a play called *Heaven's Gates, Hell's Flames*. I took special notice of a scene where one construction worker shared his faith with another, on their lunch break. The second man became a believer. Suddenly, the section of the building they were sitting on broke. The two men fell and died. Yet even the man who had only just given his life to the Lord went to heaven. It showed me that I didn't need to strive to please God.

Another scene scared me – a young woman had just been dumped by her boyfriend. She was not in a good place and decided to take her own life. At this point, the lights turned red, and thumping, frightening drums sounded. A dark figure, representing the devil, came onto the stage, grabbed the girl and dragged her away by her hair. The scene ended with a maniacal laugh. I've never forgotten it.

That scene made me more aware than ever before that I needed to make a decision to follow Jesus for myself, and not just because my parents believed. My family's faith was not going to save me. Everyone has to meet their maker by themselves. Those who don't know Jesus end up spending eternity in hell with the devil. Who would want that?

When the play ended and the MC gave an altar call, I responded. I knew I was already a Christian, but I needed to make my faith more real, more personal.

I told one of the counsellors there that I was scared that God wouldn't love me if I wasn't completely good. He said, "God's not like that," that God's love for me is unconditional. God was beginning to unravel the lies I'd believed about myself; the lies that said the abuse I'd suffered was my fault.

From then on, I attended church every week with Clarissa. I made friends with everyone at that church. The pastors, a husband and wife team, were so honest, genuine and oozing with love. They were good shepherds. They welcomed me straight away. I also began attending youth group each Friday night. We all used to go to Hog's Breath Café afterwards. And after church on Sundays, we used to hang out at various beaches and parks. One day, I explained the passage about the mustard seed to a friend called Jason, and encouraged him to read it. A few months later, he asked me to come to his baptism.

Afterwards, the pastor asked if anyone else wanted to be baptised. I said I did. I'd already been baptised as a little girl but I wanted to renew my commitment.

Making the decision to follow Jesus for myself was liberating. God started working to heal me of the effects of the abuse as soon as I gave my life to him.

Imagine being Father God and knowing that your precious child has been sexually abused by both an evil spirit and a rogue boyfriend. It must be horrible for him. I'm sure he feels more anger, more sadness at what's happened to me than I do.

False Teaching and Slut Shaming

One Saturday night, Abbi from youth group had a party. She invited all the church friends and some of us stayed the night. I don't know why I did this, but I hooked up with one of the guys.

We didn't do anything more than I was comfortable with. He was respectful and stopped when I asked. But I regretted it afterwards.

I believe God allowed this to happen so that I could see the difference between consensual fooling around and rape. What Samson had done was wrong, whereas Michael stopped when I asked.

Even though I regretted what I'd done, I'm thankful to God for using this mistake to help me understand the differences between consent and rape.

One evening, Billy dropped Holly and I home from youth group. From age sixteen, I suffered from claustrophobia. I could usually control it quite well, but that night, in the back of a windowless combi-van, in the dark, I had a full-on panic attack. I felt trapped. I couldn't breathe properly.

I asked Holly if we could swap spots. She didn't believe me at first, saying, "Oh sure," sarcastically, thinking I was just making an excuse to sit next to Billy, because all us girls had a crush on him. Thankfully, Billy believed me. As soon as I sat in the front seat, my breathing returned to normal and I calmed right down.

Billy had the back of his combi set up like a lounge/bedroom with drawn curtains, a mattress on the floor and couches to sit on. There were no seat belts. I now know my freakout was due to rape related post-traumatic stress disorder (PTSD). I was triggered; the van's set up subconsciously reminding me of Samson's room.

The following day at school, I had an episode where I felt like the walls were closing in on me. It really scared me, so I asked a friend to pray that the claustrophobia would go away. I felt my sense of panic go away completely as she prayed. Peace rushed through me and I knew I was healed of the claustrophobia. And I've even been caving since!

I loved my youth group, but I did not like the head leader, Jasper, and his double standards about sexuality. He had this stupid idea that us girls had to be "perfect" little Christians who didn't ever flirt with boys, nor have any sexual desires at all. Yet this leader flirted with all the girls, all the time, even some that were much younger than him.

Girls were expected to be passive, submissive and asexual towards men, while simultaneously being ready to give our husbands sex whenever they might want once we were married; marriage being something we were expected to do. We weren't even supposed to hug our male friends, even though hugging your friends is completely normal, even vital, especially for teenagers.

Crazy, isn't it? There is no switch we can suddenly flick when we get married, making us go from not wanting sex to suddenly being horny nymph wives.

One day at youth group Sarah warned me, "Be careful with Jasper. He likes girls." Jasper was there and he nodded his consent to this, showing that he did like young girls.

The following week, I confronted Jasper about this, asking, "You don't like me, do you?"

He answered, "Of course not, you're half my age! You shouldn't assume that I like you like that. I'm your leader."

But his words did not match his actions. Why nod assent to Sarah's warning, then tell me off for confronting him about this? He clearly had some issues, but instead of dealing with them, he projected them onto me. I was astounded by Jasper's behaviour, and left wondering what I had done wrong, when I hadn't done anything wrong.

I'm noticing a pattern here; men who do the wrong thing don't like being called out, especially not by brave young women, so they turn our confrontations into something they aren't, feign offence, then walk off in an offended huff to cover their tracks. So deceitful.

Jasper also used to (probably deliberately) misread my hugs, sexualising my affection for my male friends, to the point where he said he was "afraid" to hug me in case I meant it "the wrong way". He started a rumour about me, warning the boys against me by saying I was too sexual and telling them not to hug me. I was labelled by him as the youth group "slut" and "flirt".

It was so hurtful and humiliating. Why deliberately shame one of your young people? It's just wrong. And not just in a moral sense. It was also untrue. I was neither of those things.

As you can imagine, this slut shaming compounded my already present traumas. I began to blame myself for *all and any* inappropriate behaviour from guys, because now my youth leader was calling me a slut, so seventeen-year-old me thought it must therefore be true.

As a result of internalising all these lies, I now took on all the blame for what Samson had done. I was overly cautious about how I behaved around boys and hyper-vigilant about how I dressed in case I "turned someone on".

I learned that I couldn't call men's inappropriate behaviour out because it would just get thrown back in my face.

One evening after youth group, Jasper dropped me and one of the guys home. He had a lingerie catalogue on the floor of his car.

I asked him why he had that, and his answer was, "Oh, for when I get a wife."

I said, "Oh," as if I understood.

What was there to understand? A youth leader, a single man in his early thirties, who was meant to be leading by example and showing us kids how to happily have sexual purity, was using lingerie catalogues as porn, and leaving them in the car he drove kids home in.

What did that say to the boys? That looking at porn and objectifying women was OK?

I reported him, and he was given two weeks off to sort himself out, then he was allowed back; leading young girls. He should have been dismissed.

Sometimes Jasper went on, "missions," or so he called them. He'd have girlfriends while on mission. When he came back, he didn't talk about what God had done. Instead, he talked about his girlfriends and about staying in the best hotels. That's not Christian mission! That's a worldly Westerner's holiday!

One night, the leaders ran some sex education sessions, one for the girls and one for the boys.

Instead of teaching us why waiting for marriage was important and healthy for us, and giving us the Bible passages to back this up, our leader gave a slide show of girls dressed in different clothes, then asked us if what these models were wearing was modest enough or not. If we disagreed with her, she subtly shamed us.

She didn't teach us how to set and keep boundaries. Nor did she teach us about consent. Instead, she made it seem like, if a guy got turned on by us, it was our fault for "tempting him" with our clothing choices. We were made to feel guilty for just being attractive young women, as if our natural God-given beauty, which we didn't choose, meant we were deliberately turning guys on.

I was especially the target for this rubbish because I have big boobs. I felt even more pressured than the other girls to "dress properly" because guys did notice me, everywhere I went, no matter what I wore. I'm not really sure how guys noticing me, even if I was wearing a daggy pair of trackies, was my fault. I didn't ask for this beauty, or these large breasts. I should not have been made to feel ashamed of my own body!

The female leader in question ought to have explained that our beauty was a gift, and taught us how to guard it. She also should have taught us that boys are responsible for their own responses to us, and that if they can't control themselves, that's their fault, not ours.

Later that night, one of the girls confessed publicly to us that her uncle molested her when she was younger. Rather than taking this opportunity to explain consent to us, our leader very briefly comforted the girl, then went straight back into telling us what we could and could not wear. It made it seem like us wearing "the wrong thing" was more of a sin than rape.

This had a very bad effect on me, compounding the trauma yet again, and cementing the mindset of self-blame I already had. I was dropped in a box called "shameful" and blamed for being there.

ACT 3

The Warrior Finds Ways to Express her Unquenchable Spirit

An urgent sounding melody with a driving beat plays, and The Warrior dance fights to it, trying to find her rhythm, trying to find her way through the darkness...

CHAPTER 15

Moving to Tasmania

The Promised House

A few weeks after I finished school, we left NSW for Tasmania. Dad hadn't been able to secure a job in Many Waters County, so he and Mum discussed where else in Australia we could move to that would have better job prospects for him *and* would be a nice place to live. Dad had always wanted to live somewhere near both mountains and the sea, so he and Mum chose Hobart.

Soon after, we were packing up our belongings and preparing for the long drive to Melbourne to catch the ferry.

For years, Mum and Dad had rented; moving from house to house at the whim of the landlords. Mum got absolutely jack of it and cried out to the Lord to provide them with a house they could call their own. Not long after this, Mum distinctly heard God tell her he'd provide them with a house that would be theirs, but that she would need to wait for the right time.

Mum clung to this promise. Even when it seemed impossible, she believed.

Within the first two weeks of being in Tasmania, Mum and Dad had found THE house. After looking at several houses, Mum and Dad settled on the house they still live in in Mountain Vista; a beautiful, functional home, surrounded by fruit trees, with a nice big deck.

As soon as we walked up the driveway and saw the deck and the mini orchard, we knew. Mum said, "This is it," before we'd even gone inside.

We bought a dog from the dog's home soon after settling into our new home. We looked at several dogs before finding Abijah; a little tan and white Border Collie. He jumped when he saw us, and wagged his tail. Mum says he chose us!

Candace said, "I want this one Mum."

Mum wanted to sleep on it before we made the final decision, but Candace already knew. She was in tears, saying, "But Mum, I want Abijah! What if someone else buys him?"

Dad got an inquiring expression on his face, and said, "Did you say his name is Abijah?" Then, "We'd better go and get him then! He's the prophet's dog!"

"Yes!" exclaimed Candace, and we went back to adopt Abijah.

The promise of the house and the fulfilment of it are not the only miracles I've witnessed. There are many.

One evening when Dad was driving home from work, another vehicle went through a red light and struck the side of our car, sending Dad spinning out of control across two lanes of traffic.

Amazingly, our car landed on the footpath the right way up, and Dad was barely hurt. Dad left the battered car where it was on the footpath, and walked the rest of the way home. Thankfully, a police officer kindly organised a tow truck to collect our poor, damaged car.

Dad didn't know how to acquire a new family car, since he didn't have the money. He prayed about it and felt God leading him to trust Him for the money.

A cheque arrived in the mail. The woman who had caused the accident had decided to send us some money to help us. Then, soon after, more money turned up in the mailbox timely gifts from church friends who didn't even know about the accident. When my parents added all this unexpected money up, they found that the amount needed for our next car was provided in full by God. Mum and Dad didn't need to pay a cent out of their own pockets.

Once, Mum and Dad had booked a family holiday, and about a week before going, a heap of bills came in, so Dad said we wouldn't be able to afford to go on holiday anymore.

Mum replied, "But that's not fair! We've been saving for ages for this trip. The girls are looking forward to it."

Mum started praying. A few days later, the money we needed turned up in the letterbox. They never did find out who it was from.

Another time, a few household items broke all at once. Mum worked out that in order to replace them; we'd need a certain amount of money. My parents didn't have that amount, so Mum prayed the money in.

Unbeknownst to my parents, a couple from church had just recently come into an inheritance. They wanted to tithe their inheritance money to someone who really needed it, and when they prayed about it, God said to give it to us.

The gift was about $200 more than what Mum had calculated was necessary to buy the items, but when she went shopping, the cost of all the items was exactly equal to Mum's original amount, plus the $200.

And a few months after arriving in Tasmania, Dad found work in a library. It was good for him to finally have another job.

God always provides what we need. Sometimes he does it in unexpected ways. Yet the prayers still get answered.

CHAPTER 16

Another Nightmare Boyfriend

I applied and was accepted to do a Fine Arts Diploma at university. I learned lithography, screen printing, etching, aquatint, paper making, drawing, and how to run a small art business.

Me and my family also became regular members of the local church and I joined the youth group.

In the middle of 2001, I met a boy called Phil while travelling on the bus. We became friends, he taught me guitar and came to our house to visit me. He was happy to talk to all my family, including my parents, which was a nice change from Samson's isolating behaviour.

During my fourth guitar lesson with him, he asked me to be his girlfriend and I said yes. The following are reconstructed diary entries from our three-year relationship.

Jules' Diary aged 19-22, 2001-2003

July 22nd 2001

Phil and I had our first official date. We went into town, looked in the shops, had lunch in the park. It was good. We get on well and we have a lot in common.

July 27th

I was at Phil's house, and we were cuddling in his room, when he pulled me onto his bed, lay on top of me and started kissing me. I was kissing him back for a while but then I started crying. He asked what was wrong and I asked him to get off me, so he did. He said, "Too much too soon?" Yes.

I said I needed to slow down physically and he said that was OK. I hope he sticks to it.

July 28th

I broke up with Phil. Something about him is scaring me. I'm not sure what. I cried when I told Mum, because I do really like him, but something doesn't feel right. I can't put my finger on it.

July 30th

Phil rang me a couple of times today to ask if I was sure about the break up. I'm not sure now myself.

3 p.m.

I rang him to say that I'd made a mistake, and could we get back together. He said yes. He's really happy.

Went over to his house later this afternoon. We were hanging out in the lounge room when he said, "I really like you."

I said, "I love you too."

I'm not sure that I do love him, but I felt pressured to say it, like there was some kind of compulsion on me. He didn't seem happy about me saying it so soon, and asked if I was sure. I wish I hadn't said it now.

July 31st

Had another date with Phil. He was already in town and I caught the bus in to meet him. The bus was ten minutes late, so I was late too. I don't have a mobile so I couldn't ring him. When I got to our meeting place, he had a big scowl on his face. He barked at me that I'd stood him up, and I explained that the bus had been late.

He kept blaming me, saying that I should have made the bus driver go faster, and that if I had of been ready earlier, the bus would have been on time. How can I control the bus driver or the traffic?

Finally, he calmed down and stopped yelling at me, and we had our date. But he was scowling whenever there was a pause in the conversation, and I felt that he was pretty much angry at me all day for something I couldn't control.

August 5th

Dad warned me about Phil, saying that his mum had told him that Phil could be very controlling. I didn't know that. I don't really think it's true. I mean, he seems so nice.

August 10th

Today, when I said I was thinking of going on Centrelink payments because I don't earn enough at work, Phil told me not to, saying, "I don't want you to be on Centrelink."

I asked him why and he said he just didn't want me to deal with the hassle of it. I thought it was nice that he was thinking of my well-being, but still, isn't it my choice?

Then he tried to convince me to quit my job, by saying that Helga wasn't a very good manager (not true). Then he said, "I don't want you to work because I can look after you."

I didn't feel comfortable with that, so I told him I want to keep my job. He was mostly respectful of that, except that for a few minutes he continued to try and convince me that Helga wasn't a good manager and that I'd be better off by letting him look after me.

I said, "I'm not quitting my job Phil. It's my first job and I really like it."

After that, he acted like he'd lost a game and was mad about it. It's not a game, it's my life, and I'm allowed to run it.

August 22nd

Things have been pretty good for a while. Phil hasn't been mean or angry in a few weeks. I like kissing him. He doesn't demand that I kiss him, like Samson did. It's a relief.

We had a lovely time at a concert in town. He said he'd take me backstage to meet the band, then he didn't. I was a bit disappointed because I was really looking forward to meeting them. But I didn't complain because I'm trying to work on being easier to get on with. Sometimes people say I'm too much, or I complain too much.

August 24th

Phil's been telling me not to hang out with Dahlia. I don't know why. He said he doesn't like her. I love Dahlia. She's my best friend here in Tassie.

August 25th

Today Phil told me not to hang out with, "that Greek girl." He wouldn't say her name. I told him I'm not going to do that. As if I'm going to stop talking to Rhiannon because he told me to. And what's with saying "That Greek girl," with such venom. Is he a racist?

August 30th

Phil gets on well with my friends Lisa and Royal. I like that he gets on with them. We all had dinner together last night. He's coming with me to a friend's wedding next weekend, and Royal is going to drive us.

12th September

We went to the wedding. We had a good time. Suzanne looked beautiful!

I didn't like one thing Phil did though. One of our friends has a mental illness that makes her forget people's names. She doesn't do it on purpose, and I think part of the problem is her medication. Phil's never seemed to have an issue with it until today.

Melina couldn't remember Phil's name and he got really upset about it. He complained to Royal about it, saying that Melina was being deliberately mean and that she was ignoring him. I know he's allowed to be upset, but you should have heard the venom in his voice.

13th September

Phil rang me and started accusing me of not being a good friend to Royal. He said that she'd complained to him about me, saying that I never help out with petrol money, and that I should be more giving.

I did give Royal some money after the wedding, and I have done so beforehand too. Maybe I should have given her some more? I don't know.

Then he said that none of my friends really like me, and that they are all complaining about me to him, saying I'm a bad friend, and that I should just hang out with him.

Is it true? Am I a bad friend? Maybe I should start being more generous. I'll give Royal a bit more money.

September 17th

I went out with Dahlia, and we were having a nice time, when Phil showed up. He told me to cut my time with Dahlia short because he wanted to spend time with me. I said I wasn't going to do that, because I wanted to spend time with Dahlia, and he got upset.

I didn't listen. I wasn't going to cut my time with my best friend short.

But he kept on appearing, spying on us from around the bushes.

September 20th

I've told Phil I need a break from him. He is exhausting me.

October 1st

Phil and I went on another date and it was mostly good, but he accused me of never dressing up for him, even though I do. He said it because I had done myself up a bit in order to hand out some resumes, to try and get a job with more hours. He accused me of never focusing on him during our dates. Just *because I wanted to hand resumes out today, doesn't mean I never focus on him.*

The rest of our date was good though. We had fun looking through the shops and going to the markets.

CHAPTER 17

Things get Physical

October 20th
Things have been going well. Phil has been really loving and attentive lately, calling me beautiful, making me dinners. I feel loved.

October 30th
Phil's accusing me of cheating on him. I don't know why. I said I hadn't, but he keeps saying I flirt with boys all the time. Then he said he saw me talking to a guy this afternoon.
I was just talking to him. I wasn't flirting. Why does he think he can't trust me?

November 2nd
Phil keeps accusing me of cheating. He gets angrier every time.

November 6th
Phil hit me! He hit me really hard in the lower back. I'm crying, hiding in my room. He left in a huff.

He'd been accusing me of cheating again, getting right up in my face. He just wouldn't believe that I hadn't cheated, and his anger escalated till he got so angry he hit me.

November 11th
Phil and I were doing the dishes together at his house, and he kept telling me off for not putting them in the drying rack the right way round. I didn't think there was a right way round.

He kept picking them up, clicking his tongue and turning them around the other way, as though it were a big deal. So weird and finicky. Why does it matter?

November 15th
Phil and I were at his house doing dishes again, and he again started complaining about which way round I put them. He was even angrier than last time. What is it with him and the dishes?

November 20th
Phil did it again. The dishes thing. What is wrong with you Phil?

He kept yelling in my face about it, saying he'd told me which way round was the right way before. I mean really, they're just dishes. Get a grip!

November 21st
Phil hit me again. This time it was about the dishes. He punched me over and over in the stomach, yelling at me that I hadn't done the dishes right. Everything hurts now, including my back.

Thankfully, his family weren't home. Imagine what his mum would have said.

November 27th
Phil has been really kind lately, saying he's really sorry that I have a sore back, and that he doesn't know why it's sore. He keeps rubbing it for me and saying he thinks I might have a back problem for life now, and he's sorry it's so sore, but he'll look after me.

He keeps saying that he'll look after me, in this really calming voice. I feel like I can forget all my worries when he says it, like I'm in a bit of a trance.

6th December
I had an appointment with the physio about my back. He got me to do some exercises, and he said the problem is I have short hamstrings, and I need to stretch them out to elongate them. He asked me if I knew how it happened, because having short hamstrings doesn't usually occur unless you've over exercised or had physical force come against your stomach or pelvis.

Something in the back of my brain is screaming at me that my back pain is not from too much exercise, but I can't think of anything else I've done.

I have been walking and running a lot lately, to try and lose some weight. Phil wants me to be thinner. I guess being thinner wouldn't hurt. And I do have to bend down low to use the printing presses at uni. Maybe it's from that too. Phil did suggest it could be from that...

15th December

Phil and I were at Uni, chatting while I did some stretches for my back in the courtyard. As I was stretching, I suddenly had this thought that my back pain has something to do with something Phil did.

The thought wouldn't go away. It kept playing through my mind, even when I dismissed it.

Phil asked me what was wrong, and I said I didn't think my back problems were from using the printing presses, and he got all agitated and started trying to hurry me up. But I said I wasn't going to because I needed to do my stretches.

He got so impatient and mad that he left me in the courtyard by myself, and went inside, where he stood by the window watching me for the next ten minutes.

Saturday, 19th December

Phil asked me earlier this week if we could do something this Saturday together, so we arranged to go to the markets.

I told him that my back is really bad, and that I want to go for a swim in the pool beforehand, to help ease my pain.

He agreed.

But then, today, as we were heading into town for our market date, he started saying he didn't want to go to the pool because it would be boring for him to just sit there watching me.

I suggested he come swimming with me, but he didn't want to, said he'd just wait for me.

We got to the pool, and I had my swim. I did lots of laps to ease my back pain, and it helped, but Phil just sat there with this angry look on his face, glaring at me and mouthing for me to hurry up.

Afterwards, I met him at the stalls. He was really angry I'd taken so long. He kept saying I was selfish for putting my needs before his, that I didn't care about him, and we always had to do what I wanted first. He went on like this for 20 minutes.

Am I selfish? Should I have deferred my swim for him?

I thought I needed the swim.

Is he right about me though? Am I selfish?

22nd December

Phil and I had a special dinner at a restaurant to celebrate our six-month anniversary. The meal was nice and romantic. There were even candles.

But on the way there, he kept calling me "tight pants" and accusing me of flirting with other guys. I said I was dressing up for him, and then he started saying I was fat and ugly, and that no other man would ever want me or find me attractive. Then, in the same breath, he turned around and said, "No actually, that's not true. You are actually very beautiful and sexy. Too sexy. I'm sorry I said that, but if I don't put you down, you'll run off with someone else."

January 21st 2002

I broke up with Phil again about a week ago, and I feel really guilty about it. He has explained to me that he gets angry because his dad doesn't talk to him, and he doesn't mean to take it out on me.

Maybe I should have stayed. A lot of his friends, and mine, aren't talking to him anymore. He's only really got me and his mum and brother.

January 22nd
   Phil keeps ringing me, trying to make me take him back. He said sorry for being mean. I don't know what to do.

January 24th
   I got back with Phil. I still love him. I was finding being without him hard. And he is so sad without me.

February 1st
   Phil's been calling me beautiful again, and making me dinner. I think he loves me.

February 4th
   Phil started calling me a bad person, telling me that no one would ever want me. He keeps trying to get me to stop hanging out with my friends, and it's becoming even more frequent than before. I know he loves me, because he tells me so, calls me beautiful and makes me dinner, but I don't think I can take this much longer.

February 5th
   Phil said to me, "You'll never find anyone else to put up with you. You're so weak; you'll never survive without me."
   Is it true? Am I weak? Am I hard to deal with?

March 7th
   Everything's been going OK for a while. Phil hasn't been mean to me for about a month. I've decided to stay with him. Maybe it'll be OK. Maybe he'll get better...

June 7th

Phil and I went rock climbing today, then tonight, we went to a concert. Some of my friends were there.

I kept stretching my hamstrings, because they were really stiff, and my back was hurting a lot, and one of my friends asked, "Why didn't you stay home and ask Phil to massage you, if you're that sore?"

Something in me was questioning why I was so sore from just rock climbing. Something in my brain is trying to tell me that my soreness is Phil's fault.

Why? Has he done something to me?

Then, when we were leaving, he told me off for stretching in front of Mary. He told me not to tell people about my back problems. He seemed quite worried that anyone would know. I don't know what's wrong with him.

August 15th

We were making scones at Phil's house. He kept on fussing and complaining that I wasn't doing it right. Then he said, "You're so stupid. Can't you even make scones? You won't make a very good wife."

September 16th

Phil's started accusing me of studying too much, saying I don't spend enough time with him. Then he said that I put my studies before him. No I don't. Do I? I need to study to get my diploma.

September 18ᵗʰ

Phil's at it again. Accusing me of putting my studies before him. I feel really guilty. Am I a bad girlfriend? Should I give him more time?

I'll meet with him tomorrow to talk about it.

October 4ᵗʰ

I was meant to meet Phil on the bus so we could travel to town together for our one-year anniversary celebration. I was waiting at the bus stop, when the bus drove straight past me.

I was so scared Phil would be mad at me.

He didn't hit me, but he did go on and on about how I was late.

October 16ᵗʰ

Phil's been accusing me of cheating a lot lately, and his accusations have been escalating over the past few weeks.

Today seemed like the climax of his anger. He yelled at me that I was a slut and a whore, accusing me of cheating over and over again.

I said, "I never cheated on you." He slapped me across the face! In front of everyone!

Dahlia was in shock. She kept saying, "He hit you!" over and over.

October 18th

A day from hell

I went to Phil's house to see him, and I hadn't eaten enough all day, because he keeps telling me he wants me to be thinner. I started feeling dizzy on the way over. Then, after I'd been there awhile, he suddenly got really angry with me, started calling me fat and saying he'd kill me if I didn't get thinner!

Then he came at me with a knife, put it against my neck, saying "If you leave me, I'll kill you."

Then he cut me on my legs, shaved some of the skin off.

I am so shocked!

So much for, "Why didn't you leave him?" I can't now! He'll kill me! Help, Jesus!

CHAPTER 18

The Long Goodbye

October 20th

I did it. I finally broke up with him. He got so mad; he threw me against the wall and got right up in my face, saying, "You can't leave me. You're mine. You belong to me!"

His eyes changed colour to black. How is that normal?

I tried to get away from him, but I couldn't. I hurt my shoulder trying to get away from him.

November 4th

Phil keeps turning up at work, trying to get me to look at him. He waits around till I'm finished my shift; then comes up and asks me to hang out with him.

November 7th

Phil turned up today with a girl from uni. Then, on the bus, he kept trying to sit next to me, to tell me about his "date" with his friend from uni, even though I didn't want to talk to him.

November 19th

Phil keeps turning up at home, saying he wants to hang out. I don't know how to tell him no. I wish he'd just leave me alone.

November 25th

Phil comes into work almost every day now, then begs me to hang out with him afterwards. Because I don't always know how to say no to him, I end up going somewhere with him. I wish I didn't.

Sometimes I do say no, but he just talks me into it, or threatens to hurt me if I don't. I don't feel like I have much choice.

Some good news is that Dahlia gave me a mobile. So now I can message her if I need help; if Phil's turning up when he shouldn't.

November 26th

Phil has begun following me around town. Wherever I go, he's there.

December 1st

I was at uni after work, doing some study, when Phil turned up. He demanded I talk to him, so I walked away, got into a lift. He followed me. Rode with me up to the second floor. He called me a bitch in front of the other people in the lift.

I got out of the lift on the second floor, and thankfully, he didn't come with me. But 15 minutes later, when I came back down to the first floor, he was there, waiting for me.

He asked what I was doing now, and demanded he come with me. I had to look at the art in the gallery with him staring over my shoulder.

December 17th

I was about to walk down to youth group when Phil turned up. He asked what I was doing, and he demanded I let him come with me. He followed me out the door, then kept walking with me down the street, even though I told him not to, several times.

And all the way along, he complained that I don't let him do anything with me anymore.

Then, when we got to youth group, I told him to go away and that he wasn't to come in with me. Finally got rid of him.

December 20th

Phil says that he told Chris I wouldn't let him come with me to youth group that night. Apparently, Chris said, "That's not how it should be."

I feel so guilty now. Maybe I should have let him come.

December 24th

Just before my shift ended, Phil turned up, asking if he could hang out with me. I said no, and told him that I had my work Christmas party on. Then he wheedled his way into coming with me, and sat there at the party acting like he was still my boyfriend.

5pm

He turned up at home, demanding that he join our Christmas Eve party. I said no, and slammed the door in his face. Then our friends told me I was rude. Everyone believes him, and thinks I'm rude. Nobody knows how awful he is to me.

January 6ᵗʰ 2003

Phil's been turning up at our house again, over and over, pretending he just wants to watch TV. One of my diaries has gone missing.

January 10ᵗʰ 2003

Mum has been asking me about Phil, saying it's weird that he keeps turning up. I said yes, he's very weird. She asked if he had done anything bad to me. I couldn't say yes, because what if he hurts me more if he finds out I told someone?

And what if Mum and Dad believe him, not me? What if they say I should have submitted to him?

January 13ᵗʰ 2003

I was in town again, waiting for the bus home, when Phil turned up and demanded, "I want you to marry me". I said no, because I don't love him, and he got all sad and said, "You could grow to love me."

Wow! Dude, I broke up with you. Which part of that did you not get?

January 27ᵗʰ 2003

I was at my friend Ella's house, when she pulled out my missing diary. Most of the pages were stuck together with glue.

Ella opened the bits that were not stuck together and showed them to me. Pages from another diary of mine had been stuck into this one; and my own words had been used to accuse me. There were written accusations against me in Phil's writing.

I was shocked! Even though I already knew who did this, I asked Ella, "Who would do this?!" And she said, "Phil."

On the cover, magazine letters formed the word "slut". Oh my God, help! He's a psycho!

I took the diary home. I didn't know what to do. I hid it. I didn't even want to show Mum. I didn't even pray.

January 28th

Mum found the diary. She asked me what on earth was going on. I told her that it was Phil; that Ella had found it in her letterbox. Mum went quiet, shocked. She suggested I go to the police. I told her I can't, because I'm scared he'll hurt me more if he finds out.

Mum prayed for me, then I prayed for protection over our family, our house, our car, our church, and even the area.

I want to go to the police, but I just don't feel like I can.

I don't feel safe.

January 30th

Phil has left me alone for the last couple of days. My prayers must be working.

February 4th

I still haven't heard from Phil, thank goodness. He has finally left me alone. Thank you, Lord. Please let my safety continue.

February 14th

Phil's started messaging me again. I'm ignoring him.

February 17th

Phil won't stop messaging me. I told him to leave me alone or I'll go to the police. I said I'd block him if he didn't stop.

February 20ᵗʰ

Phil hasn't messaged these last three days. But I don't trust him not to do it again.

I went to the police. The officer told me that the only thing they can do is put a restraining order on him, and she didn't think that was very effective.

So I didn't put a restraining order on him.

I wish I had though.

After this, Phil seemed to get the message and left me alone. I didn't really start to relax until around May. Then I thought it was over, but he had one last try.

At the end of December 2003, I was at the beach playing volleyball when I got a text from Phil out of the blue, saying, "Hey, what are you up to today? It's a beautiful day."

I could tell from the way he put it that he was fishing to try and get me to agree to him joining me. I replied, "I'm playing volleyball. Yes, it is a nice day. Why are you texting me? Goodbye."

He sent one more text, and I said, "I blocked you. Where did you get my new number from?"

He told me he got it from a friend, so I said, "Don't contact me again. I'm blocking you now."

I didn't hear from Phil again. Eventually, in February 2004, I made one final diary entry:

I think it's done. I think he's really gone. Thank you Jesus.

After that three-year ordeal, I wasn't functioning well. I was arguing with Mum a lot, something I don't normally do, I was struggling with my studies, and I wasn't sleeping well.

One of the worst symptoms of coming out from this abusive relationship was that at the end, I believed every single lie Phil had told me. If you hear lies for long enough, you start to believe them.

A few years later I found out that those rumours about my friends not liking me weren't true. They never said such things. He made it all up to control me. He even tried controlling what I ate, calling me fat, to the point where I developed the beginnings of anorexia.

He crossed every emotional boundary I put in place. In the end, I don't know who was worse, him or Samson. Phil was emotionally blackmailing me. He even rang Breanna and complained to her about me, trying to get her on his side.

After a few months of not sleeping properly due to fear of Phil, I went to see a Christian counsellor. She demanded that I kneel on the floor and say a forgiveness prayer, which I clearly didn't mean. She didn't acknowledge I'd been abused, nor did she validate my pain. All she did was demand I forgive, right then and there, then shamed me for, "not forgiving fast enough." That's not how forgiveness works.

That counselling session did more harm than good. It made me shut up about Phil and what he'd done, and it caused me to begin to minimise his wrongs, to the point where I once again blamed myself for what happened to me.

Real forgiveness is a process that takes time, and your feelings about the person who hurt you have far less to do with it than your *will* to forgive. We have got to stop judging hurting people for not, "forgiving" within our own made up, impatient timelines. Real forgiveness has no timeline; it just has a goal; to move on and to be at peace.

Realising this has helped me immensely, because now I can actually work on *real* forgiveness, instead of just saying I have done so, in order to shut some hyper-religious people up and get them off my back.

A few years after this disastrous relationship, I began seeing a different counsellor. She said that what I had suffered was abuse, and that it wasn't my fault. She didn't rush me to forgive, or even mention forgiveness. Instead, she let me ask for help to move towards forgiveness when I was ready to do so. What a relief it is to finally know real forgiveness.

I used to look back and think, "Why did I put up with that?"

Fair question. But now I know the answer.

Phil used the typical abuser's tools to control me and string me along: idolise, love bomb, demand, degrade, love bomb some more, deliberately confuse, then accuse, then escalate to assault, then apologise. Then love bomb again, and go back to demanding and degrading, inevitably leading to more abuse. The cycle went around and around, and I didn't know how to get off the scary roundabout. It was after he slapped me in public that I realised this had to stop. What he did after I broke up with him was stalking.

His behaviour showed a lack of trust and a lack of secure masculinity in *him*. It showed that *he* was the problem. *I* never was.

Five years after the fact, I was finally able to call this relationship what it was: dangerous abuse. I minimised it, internalised it and blamed myself for that long. I told no one.

Now my parents and sisters know, my husband knows and my close friends know. And everyone agrees that his behaviour was bad.

I will now walk in the truth of who I am. I am worthy of love, because I am a warrior princess made in the image of God.

CHAPTER 19

Aunty Amber and Uncle Shark

For my first solo holiday, I travelled back to NSW to visit family and friends.

I stayed four nights with Auntie Amber and her family. While I was staying with Auntie Amber, I noticed a peculiar, menacing atmosphere in the house.

Uncle Shark and Amber had an argument while I was there. He got so mad and controlling, and afterwards, he refused to speak to her for hours.

One afternoon while Uncle Shark was at work, I went into his study to find something to read. While I was looking through the bookshelves, I found some porn and a magazine about family abuse, hidden between two Christian magazines.

Then I found his diary. I felt like I was meant to see what he'd written, so I opened it. On the first page I turned to, I saw that he'd written about Amber in a way that seemed like he was idolising her: "She's my beautiful one. She's my angel."

A few pages on, he'd written, "She wants me to watch the videos with her. Ok, I will," followed by, "I want to hurt her, like in the videos." I remember thinking, "Who is this *she*?"

I knew Amber would never agree to look at porn. So who was he talking about? Clearly another woman.

The most disturbing part was that even though I knew, "she," referred to another woman, (which meant he was cheating), I also instinctively knew that, "I want to hurt her, like in the videos," was about Amber. He was admitting to wanting to hurt his own wife. It was horrifying.

I shook myself out of feeling like I was in a dream and got out of there. I never wanted to go into that study again.

That night I witnessed Uncle Shark being violent towards his own children.

They were in their room, talking and laughing when they were meant to be going to sleep. Normal kid stuff. Amber told them to be quiet, but they kept giggling.

Uncle Shark angrily rose from his chair. Then he stood in front of the kids' bedroom door, and as he stood there, his look changed from simply angry to cold and calculated, as though planning an attack.

He opened the door and entered their room, slamming the door behind him. Everything went silent. Then I heard him laying into them, heard the thwack as his hands beat them, heard their sobs and whimpers.

Again, I felt like I was in a dream. I was powerless to stop it and I knew I couldn't talk to Auntie Amber about it, in case it endangered her.

I wanted to call the police but given what happened last time I saw his violence, I thought no one would believe my witness.

So I did nothing.

I felt wretched that I did nothing, but I was frozen with fear.

A few years later, we found out the full scope of his violence.

Grandma rang Dad in tears because Amber had come over to her house covered in bruises. Grandma knew straight away Uncle Shark had hit her, and she also knew instinctively that it hadn't been the first time.

This time he'd hit her face, making the evidence that much harder to cover up.

Amber decided it was time to tell the truth. He'd been beating her for years. He even threatened to kill my cousins.

Poor Grandma was tricked by him too. He manipulated her to make her feel guilty for taking Amber's side. Grandma told Mum that she felt like her taking Amber's side was hurting the whole family. My parents had to explain that she should take Amber's side, Amber was the victim.

Amber decided to file for divorce and try for sole custody of the children. Grandma advocated for Amber to get sole custody of my cousins. However, the police officer wouldn't believe that Uncle Shark was dangerous.

Finally, a new police officer said he thought that the children should only be with their mother, because he'd observed that my cousins were afraid of their father, which likely meant Uncle Shark had done something wrong.

I'd been praying for months that someone in power would see that the children were not safe with their father. Now my prayers were being answered.

The final court ruling was that Amber should have sole custody of the children, and that Uncle Shark was not allowed to see or contact them. Amber and the children then had to flee from where they were living, because he became even more violent and manipulative, tricking their mutual friends into believing that she was the problem.

I'm so glad we got him out of our lives, and that Amber and my cousins are now free. God always prevails and goodness always wins, no matter the storms that come against us. Isn't that wonderful to know?

CHAPTER 20

A Wonderful Volunteer
Position

Happy music again swells, as the young warrior princess learns to lead.

Soon after returning home from the NSW visit, I became a volunteer with Fusion. I really enjoyed working for them. It was very rewarding, and I believe it's where God wanted me at that time.

We ran a youth café once a week, where youth could drop in and play games with their friends, do crafts, talk to youth workers and counsellors, and have afternoon tea.

I was often put on as the crafts overseer, which I really enjoyed. Once, I ran an art course for the youth, in which I taught drawing and box making. The kids seemed to really like learning observational drawing skills. I taught them how to draw what they could see, rather than what they thought their subject should look like. At the end of the course, I held an exhibition of their work. Each student received a handmade certificate.

Each Wednesday morning, I helped with the Breakfast Club at the local high school. I used to challenge myself to talk to everyone, even the kids I found it hard to talk to, and I encouraged the shy kids to join in.

Organising the daytrips was a big deal. We had to decide on dates, locations, venues, and activities. Then we had to advertise. It was my job to send out invitations, put up posters, and tell people about these trips.

One of my favourite trips was our four-wheel-driving adventure. I gave the talk that night. It was titled, "You can live an extraordinary life." I talked about Mother Teresa, Paul and Jesus, and their examples of living extraordinary lives. I said we are meant to follow their example; each of us is meant to live an extraordinary life. It was a real privilege to be able to share. Afterwards, I led two young people to the Lord.

I was really impressed with Andrea, one of our regulars. At dinner time, some of the boys were talking and laughing while we were saying grace, so she reprimanded them for being rude. Good on you girl!

Once, a few of us travelled up to Honeycomb Karst, to help out with a caving day trip. We went caving in the Honeycomb Caves. My job that day was to lead the different groups through the cave. I traversed that trail countless times that day.

Each time I led another group into the cave, I noticed something different; like the ochre boulders either side of the track, and the bright crystals glowing in the rock.

Part of my job was to show each group how to get over the stream safely, preferably without getting wet. Once, while doing so, I put my foot in the water! I laughed and said, "Don't do it like that". The kids said, "Yes Jules, we won't copy you." Everyone chuckled.

After I'd finished leading the last group back out of the cave, I got to have a go abseiling down the rock face of the cave, and into the cave's mouth via going through a waterfall! It was so exhilarating! I got wet and saw rainbows.

I also fondly remember going white water rafting on the Explorer River, and one of our rafts springing a leak. We were rowing down river next to a rocky overhang, when we all heard a hissing sound. After checking our raft, we all realised it was one of the other teams' rafts that was leaking. So we had to pull all the rafts ashore and wait while our guides deflated the leaking raft and stored it into ours. Then we had to paddle back to the visitor's centre with two teams in the one raft!

On the way back, we had a paddling race with the other teams and some of the kids jumped into the river for a swim. It was a great day.

I have so many good memories of working with Fusion. Playing games with the kids, going swimming and ten pin bowling, seeing another leader grin from ear to ear the night he led a regular day tripper to the Lord, encouraging the other leaders, laughing, talking, being silly. These were some of the best days of my life.

In 2006, I went on a mission trip to Greece with Fusion.

The funds for that trip were supplied miraculously. I hadn't been sure I could afford to go on the Eternal Arts pilgrimage in Italy, right after the Greece Mission trip, but I knew God wanted me to go, so I'd been praying the money in, yet I still didn't have enough.

I got all upset one day, worrying that I wouldn't be able to go. Dad said I should stop worrying; that I wasn't operating in faith. So I began praying in the money with a better attitude. I'd already taken on a second part time job to save up for the trip, and three jobs was out of the question. I was at the point where I had to leave it to God; a real lesson in trust.

One afternoon, I felt God tell me to ask for prayer support for the funds, so I rang our youth leader to ask him to pray more money in for me. Next morning, he rang to say he'd spoken to the parish council, and they'd agreed to sponsor me $400. A real blessing! Now I only needed another $100.

Not long after that, my grandparents gave me another $500 towards the trip, then my parents gave me another $500. Now I had more than enough.

Then I sold an artwork, and I got an order for another one.

God really provided. I went from worrying about not having enough, to having plenty.

The following week, another miracle of provision happened. My friend also wanted to go on the Greece trip, but she didn't have anywhere near enough money, so she also was praying for a miracle. As she was praying, she felt God tell her to believe for $200.

I clearly remember praying for her; God told me to pray for exactly $200 for her, and to pray it would just turn up. I hadn't known about God telling her to pray for that same amount!

The next day, she rang me to ask if I'd left $200 on her desk. When I said no, she said, "That's weird, $200 just appeared in an envelope on my desk." She'd asked around, and no one else had put it there either.

An amazing testimony. We were ready to go to Greece.

CHAPTER 21

Adventures in Greece

On the first day, we took an open air, double-decker bus tour of Athens. We saw the temples of Apollos and Zeus, and the site of the first Olympic Games. We visited Mars Hill and the Acropolis. We stood atop Mars Hill and looked out over the city, saw its plains, valleys and hills all stretched out below us. I noticed the veins of white marble in the hills, shining like satin ribbons in the sun.

Then we listened to Melvin tell us how the Apostle Paul came to this site and preached to the Athenian scholars about their "unknown god", who was really Jesus.

I vividly remember driving by a magnificent mountain range on the way to Ptolomieda for intense missions training; its towering pointed granite peaks rising sharply above us, poking the bright blue sky. Below us was a large, azure lake, surrounded by ochre boulders dotted with olive trees. We passed a little town called Larissa built atop a steep gorge and I wished we could stop. It looked so gorgeous. From the bus, I glimpsed the river, sparkling through the silvery green leaves of the surrounding trees.

Each day of training, we arose at nine a.m. for personal devotions in the garden. These were followed by group devotionals and prayers. Then after brunch, we met in the conference hall for festival training. Training always began with a talk about what God had been doing in the community. There was always a translator, because there were both Greek and English speakers present. Whoever gave the talk informed us what they perceived the community needed spiritually. We tried to plan our festivals around that information. Once the talk was finished, we prayed for the upcoming festivals, and for each other. Then we learnt festival skills, like clowning and face painting.

Each night after training, we ran festivals for the locals at a local park. I was put on bubble blowing duty, for which I wore my hand made clown costume. I loved clowning around with the children, playing silly games and showing them how to dip the big bubble wands into the bubble mixture and swirl them around to make big, beautiful bubbles.

Then we were split into three groups and each group went to minister at a different part of the nation. I was put in the Athens team.

We ran our Athenian festivals in a local park on a hillside, surrounded by poplars.

I was put on ballooning duty for these festivals. I made balloons for the kids, and I learned to speak some more Greek. Now I could talk to the kids and ask them what balloon shape they wanted. I still remember how to say, "What colour do you want?" in Greek: "Psu chroma thali?"

During our last Athens festival, I played jump rope with the locals, and ran the circus skills station. At the end of the night, the DJ turned the music up loud, and we danced the

Zorba together, Aussie missionaries and local Greeks. Round and round in a circle we went, kicking our legs high, arms linked in solidarity, yelling "Hey!"

One of my best memories is of the combined church services we attended. Local Christians from different denominations came together, and we sang worship songs in three different languages, all at once – Albanian, English and Greek. It was heavenly!

Halfway through our time in Greece, we were given a special day off. My team went Greek Island hopping. We had such a lovely time, travelling between islands on various ferries.

After our first ferry trip, we arrived at an island called Aegina, where the water was the colour of liquid sapphires. I took a walk to a local café with Anne, along the cobble stoned streets. We admired the rendered buildings built right onto the street, beautiful in their pastel shades of pink, peach and ochre, and the donkeys pulling old fashioned carts, their hooves clip-clopping on the cobblestones.

After our walk, we met back up with the rest of the team and enjoyed a special lunch at a seafood restaurant, decorated with grape vines growing from pots; their tendrils trailing down the white washed walls.

After lunch, we caught a smaller ferry to another island; a beautiful landmass with an extinct volcano sitting in its centre, surrounded by hills covered in stone pine forest. Where the forest ended, the land suddenly dropped into the clear turquoise sea via sharp cliffs.

We stopped at a small beach, sat sipping on coffee frappes. Then the boys and I went for a walk along the white marble track to the sea cliffs, where we took turns jumping off into the incredibly blue ocean.

I swam next to the cliffs and admired the fish. There was a family of rainbow fish caring for each other amongst the anemones, and further out in the deep a large school of silver perch swam above some barracudas. What a sight! The water was so clear, I could see right to the bottom!

Next, we travelled to Philippi; one of the most memorable parts of the trip.

We visited the site where the Apostle Paul and Silas were imprisoned. We saw the magisterial courthouse where Paul and Silas were tried. We stood atop the actual jail cell they were imprisoned in, while Melvin read out the story from the Bible. Then we sang, "My chains fell off, my heart was free, I rose, went forth and followed thee." What a place to declare God's freedom!

Then we travelled to Lydia's River; the site where Paul met the lady Lydia, a sacred site where an outdoor church has been built right onto the river bank. It has a baptismal fountain carved out of marble, tiered marble pews and a carved marble pulpit, all surrounded by leafy green trees under which the fast-running river flowed. It was so beautiful!

After resting at the church awhile, I walked along the riverbank. I saw tall weeping willows casting their cascading leaves into the water, as though washing their green hair.

Behind the outdoor church was another little church, made of white marble and surrounded by a leafy walled garden. I entered the garden through the golden gates and walked along the white marble path leading to the front doors of the church. Inside, it was cool and quiet, with pictures of the saints adorning the pink walls.

Next, we drove to Corinth, where we met one of the local pastors at the site of the ancient city. While sitting among the fallen pillars of the ruined pagan temple, he read to us from 1 Corinthians 11, the part about not eating food dedicated to idols. It was amazing to have him explain the cultural context of this passage while right there at the site.

Afterwards, we walked through the site and saw the jail, the basilica, and the remnants of the hill-top temple.

At the foot of that hill, the pastor gave a sermon on 2 Corinthians 11, the part about women needing to cover their heads. I'd always wondered about this passage. "Surely it's cultural and doesn't apply to women today?"

We learned that ancient Corinth was a busy seaside port, where sailors from all over the world gathered to purchase supplies. Afterwards, they visited taverns and got drunk, then wandered up to the temple to engage with prostitutes.

The temple was dedicated to the goddesses Aphrodite, and worship involved men engaging in intercourse with the temple prostitutes. The baser the sexual acts, the higher the worship, or so they thought. As a result, the sailors often enacted their worst sexual fantasies onto the prostitutes, using "high worship to Aphrodite" as an excuse for their violent behaviour. Raping and assaulting these women was common, and public intercourse was prized, especially anal sex, which was meant to somehow bring fertility to the people of Corinth.

These women did not have a good life. They had to constantly give themselves to men who didn't love or deserve them, many of whom wanted to hurt them. They weren't allowed to say no, either. There were punishments for them if they refused or resisted.

Enduring this daily abuse was not the limit to their degradation, however. Their heads were shaved to mark them as temple prostitutes. They were made to wear simple, unflattering hessian dresses, and they weren't given any other clothes. They weren't allowed to look pretty. Their "purpose" was literally to be a sex object. They also had an arrow carved into their left sandals, meaning that wherever they trod, men could find them by their marked footsteps, and follow them back to the temple. They were literally marked out as fodder for male perversion.

Other Corinthian women didn't fare much better. They were married off and used as breeding machines. Despite this, many Corinthian wives judged the prostitutes as unworthy, and thought of themselves as superior. It was common for them to taunt the prostitutes with nasty names.

Not long after Paul started a house church movement in Corinth, some of the prostitutes joined the family of God, and became regulars at church meetings. Some even started their lives anew, marrying good men or being given more rewarding work with the church.

Yet the other women still judged and mocked them.

Paul's instructions that women within the church wear head coverings stopped these women from teasing the newly converted prostitutes for their shaven heads. If all women had to wear head coverings, they would all look the same, making it that much harder to distinguish between (ex) prostitutes and other women. The whole reason Paul told the women to cover their heads was to stop the bullying, and to help all the women in Corinth love each other as equals.

His command was never meant as a blanket rule to cover all women. It was for a specific church movement within a specific city, for an appointed time in history. It was so good to learn this, and to finally understand this passage properly.

CHAPTER 22

The Delights of Italy

From Kalamata, we took a ferry to Italy. I enjoyed standing on the deck, watching the ochre cliffs of Greece slide by, their grandness reflected in the green sea.

We arrived at Andorra, its stark ochre cliffs plunging into the waves. After disembarking, we caught a train to Florence, where we stayed three nights in the beautiful Hotel Linda; a two story, traditional Italian building built right onto the street front. Inside, it was plush, with red carpets, decorative, wrought iron banisters, and a fancy mezzanine overlooking the reception area.

Florence was beautiful and romantic. On our first day, we explored the huge, ornate cathedral in the central square. The outside walls were highly decorated, with intricate marble sculptures of angels, saints, gargoyles, Jesus and Father God. I was struck by the way the craftsmen had gradated the tones of marble to make a pattern; brown, then pink, then grey, then green then white, repeated over and over.

The front door was large and oaken, adorned with brass knockers with twisted pillars standing either side of it. Inside, it was quiet, with a hushed and reverent atmosphere. The space was vast. There was approximately fifteen metres between floor and ceiling. The floors were made of different coloured marbles, the walls were adorned with carvings and sculptures, and the ceiling was painted with choirs of angels singing praises to the Most High. A huge pipe organ sat behind the marble altar, and here and there about the place, candelabras stood on white tables; their tapered cream candles lit with golden flames giving off a warm light.

We also walked over the Ponta Vecchio, the famous bridge crossing the green Arno River, perfect reflections mirroring back at us from the depths.

Then we took a city bus tour to a beautiful town called Fiesole, on the hill above Florence. We disembarked at the lookout halfway up. From there we spied the Arno River and the Basilica. The whole valley was bathed in golden light as the sun descended. We climbed to the top of the hill and came to a tiny chapel. It was beautiful and calm inside. We walked out onto a veranda decorated with marble archways, with stairs leading down to a little garden. It was cool and shady there; a welcome respite from the heat.

Then we walked along a path that led to a meadow overlooking the fields of Tuscany; golden wheat and yellow green grass making way to distant fields of violet lavender, all shining hazy rose in the setting sun.

On the bus back to our hotel, the driver had to brake suddenly, so I said, "Far out!" Then I heard an Italian woman cry, "Mamma Mia!" We both looked at each other in surprise. Then we started laughing. I thought "Mamma Mia" was just a phrase used in movies. I didn't know Italians really say it. The Italian woman clearly thought the same thing about Australians saying "far out".

On our last day we visited the Florence Museum, where we studied the famous sculpture of David, saw the painting of Venus by Botecelli and enjoyed a musical instrument exhibition, where instruments from all over the world, and from throughout time, were displayed. I liked the giant serpentine, the display of violins throughout the ages and the funny looking harpsichord, such a weird instrument.

After our lovely time in Florence, we caught a train to Rome, where we stayed in a convent.

Everything in Rome was so exciting. I'd never seen anything like it. There was so much history.

On our first day, we did a walking tour of the Coliseum. We learned some really interesting facts about how it was built, and we heard some awe inspiring stories.

It was a bloody place, known for its gladiatorial battles, animal hunts, and executions. To begin with, the gladiatorial battles were used as a way for the rich to honour their dead. A few hundred years later, Emperor Augustus decided to use the gladiatorial battles as a form of free public entertainment, in order to gain votes.

Things got even worse when Emperor Nero took charge. He began punishing Christians for their faith by sentencing them to fight in the arena. Because they were not trained gladiators, like the fighting men that came before them, their chances of survival were very slim.

These bloody spectacles were finally stopped as a result of Telemachus, a monk visiting Rome in 391 AD. He saw thousands of people entering the Coliseum, heard them cheering, and decided to follow them inside to see what was going on.

He was appalled by what he saw. As he watched, he kept feeling that he needed to put a stop to the fight. When the Holy Spirit rose up in him, he stood up and called out, "Stop, Stop!"

Quietly at first, then louder and louder, until everyone, including the emperor, could hear him. Then he turned to the emperor and said, "I beseech you emperor, we must put a stop to this."

His boldness got the emperor's attention, and the emperor began to listen. But the crowd were having none of it.

Finally, Telemachus jumped over the wall separating the seating area from the arena, and stood between two gladiators, pushing them apart, saying, "Stop, stop! This is your brother! This is your brother!" In response, the crowd stoned him to death.

Telemachus' martyrdom so impressed the emperor, he decided to put a stop to the battles by officially banning them.

The life and death of a man who wanted to show people that they were brothers in Christ was the catalyst that stopped one of the most barbaric customs in history.

We also visited the St Calixtus Catacombs, where many saints were buried in shared graves; saints who had been martyred for their faith. It was so inspiring, as was the Vatican City. We saw lots of marble sculptures in the sculpture hall, the tapestries in the royal tapestry hall and the hand drawn maps in the map room. Then we visited the Sistene Chapel, where all my favourite Bible stories were painted on the ceiling. I really liked the picture of Judith slaying Holofernes; it's a story from the Apocrypha.

As I stood looking up, I felt the power of God rain down on me, so awe inspiring were those paintings!

Next we visited the grand cathedral, with its huge entryway, its giant painted dome, its huge altar made of carved mahogany, and the beautiful blown glass sculpture of a phoenix rising from the ashes above it, made from fine strands of red and gold filigree.

We climbed the stairs to the mezzanine, saw the mosaics made of real gold and lapis lazuli. Then we climbed the spiral stairs to the top of the dome, where we looked out upon the city of Rome. What a view!

We also saw the Trevi Fountain, threw coins in for fun.

When it was time to go, I walked back to the hostel, collected my luggage and checked out, then walked to the train station where I promptly lost my way. I walked backwards and forwards, trying to find my way to the right platform.

I went to the help desk, but I couldn't speak Italian and the lady on the desk couldn't speak English, so I was stuck. I was starting to feel worried, so I prayed I'd make it to the right platform on time. Finally, I found someone who could speak English, and they showed me to the correct platform. I wasn't going to miss the train to the airport after all.

At the airport, I ran into more trouble. I was sure I'd booked a flight back to Athens airport, where my flight back to Australia was leaving from next morning. But when I looked in my bags, my ticket wasn't with me. Fortunately, the lady at the service desk could speak English. The news was bad, though. Apparently, I hadn't actually booked a flight. But she was able to book me on the nine p.m. flight that night. Thankfully, I had the money. I'd had a feeling I needed to save a good portion of money for the return journey, but I hadn't known why. Thank goodness I listened to God's leading, or I'd have been stuck in Rome.

I made it safely back home with no more hiccups. God saved the day yet again.

When I got back to Tasmania, my youth group held a combined event in my honour. I talked about my experiences, and shared some testimonies and a slide show. Then we had a party.

It felt really special to be honoured like this.

CHAPTER 23

The Warrior Grows

In 2005, I became a church youth leader. Mostly, it was fun, challenging and rewarding. I have many more good memories of this time than I do bad ones. The bad things were difficult at best and traumatic at worst, but they will never take away from the beautiful, fun memories of our good times together.

Joy was always present, even in the midst of real struggles.

I really enjoyed one particular combined youth camp at White Beach. We were split up into small groups for our Bible studies, and I was put in a group with Yvanne, Miles, Andy, Janelle and Robson.

Our group was such a mix. Yvanne was quite scientific in her approach. It resonated with me when she said, "The more you know about science and how the world was made, the more you believe in God." Miles asked some really pertinent questions; the ones everyone else was too afraid to ask. Andy was pretty forceful about his political views, even though he wasn't old enough to vote yet. Janelle was a quirky, deep thinker, and I understood everything through my faith and my creativity. All these different ways of understanding the world made for really interesting discussions.

One morning during one of these camps, I went for a walk along a pine needle strewn path, through the woods to the beach. In between two pine trees stood a little, rustic, wooden gate with a heart shape carved into it. That morning, the sunlight was shining pale gold through the trees at just the right angle to illuminate the top of the gate and cause the carved heart to glow. A beautiful illustration of God's love.

The most significant camp for many of us, (and definitely for me), was the first "Stand Strong" conference. One of our leaders choreographed two dances for it, and both dance teams performed them to live music on the first night of the conference. I was one of the dancers. Being part of the dance teams helped me grow in confidence.

I was also asked to do a series of paintings as backdrops for the band. I felt honoured to be asked.

After one significant sermon, Henry, our leader, suddenly grabbed the microphone and said, "Someone here has been sexually abused."

I had not told a soul about Samson, and only Mum, Dad and Breanna knew about the demonic assault. I started crying, then couldn't stop. Deep sobs wrenched out of me. I went forward for prayer, and fell on the floor, sobbing. Finally, I was able to let some of it go.

The leader prayed for me to be freed from a spirit of rejection. I heard Yvanne say, "He can't hurt you anymore Jules, he can't hurt you anymore."

I really needed that opportunity to admit to the others what had happened to me. I didn't tell them the whole story, partially because I hadn't yet remembered everything. But I told them enough to let some more of it go.

Next morning, Henry gave a talk on God as Father. He asked one of the guys to give out hugs to those who felt they needed a hug from Father God, as a physical representation. I needed that hug! God really moved during that conference. He touched a lot of people and changed many hearts, attitudes and minds. It was ground-breaking for some of us.

Every Friday evening we met for our regular Bible studies, discussion groups and worship times.

In 2006, things began to go wrong in the youth group. Here are some reconstructed diary entries about that.

Jules Diary, age 26, 2006

February 14th 2006
Henry decided to ask Lorelei to be a leader too, so that there's more than one senior female leader, (me).
I think it's a good idea. I like Lorelei.

February 28th
Henry and Lorelei are now going out. I'm happy for them, but I'm not sure it's a good match. Something about their relationship is ringing alarm bells for me.

March 7th
Henry gave a sermon that just seemed off. I don't know why, but I just didn't feel comfortable with it.
His sermon was on Potiphar's wife, and what happened with Joseph. He praised Joseph for his strength in resisting Potiphar's wife, saying that Joseph could have taken her up on

her tempting offer to sleep with him, but instead, he fled from temptation. He made it seem like Joseph liked her advances, and was getting turned on, but stopped himself from saying yes. And he used this to say that all the boys present could also resist sexual temptation, no matter how enticing the offer may be.

He made it sound like boys always want sex, even if it's demanded of them, and that boys never want to say no.

Henry's view doesn't seem right. I read through the passage then and there, and it seems to me like she wasn't offering sex to Joseph, but demanding it. It didn't seem like Joseph had much choice.

March 8th

Aha! I've got it! I know why I didn't like Henry's sermon.

Because it isn't Biblical, and neither is it true.

Contrary to popular belief, not all boys want sex. And even though most do, they want consensual, happy sex, not sex demanded of them from someone else's nasty wife.

It was wrong of Henry to make it seem as though it isn't masculine to not want sex. It was wrong of him to make it seem like Potiphar's wife just asked Joseph. She tried to force herself on him, and boys don't like that any more than girls do. I think he ran from her because he was scared, not because he was trying not to say yes.

It makes me worry that if any of our boys have been sexually assaulted, they may now think it wasn't assault because they, "ought to have wanted sex," with those women, and that they are somehow at fault for not saying no. And worse, that if they didn't want it, didn't feel desire for it at all; that somehow means they aren't "real men".

I mean, maybe I'm reading far too much into this. Henry often says I do that.

But I just don't feel comfortable with the effect this bit of false teaching may have had on our boys, no matter how accidental it was on Henry's part. I can't help it. I care for our kids as though I'm their big sister.

March 24th

Lorelei and I have been hanging out. She's bought me lunch a few times. She keeps complaining about Henry, saying he doesn't understand her, that he demands things of her and that he doesn't seem committed. I told her not to worry. I know Henry well, and I know he just needs a bit more time to feel committed to her. I said he was unlikely to be demanding on purpose, and that she should talk to him about that. She agreed, but she was muttering to herself about him not listening.

I love Lorelei, and I hope she and Henry work it out.

March 28th

Lorelei's been complaining about Henry again, accusing him of all sorts of really minor things. Henry told me that she makes things up about him.

I really don't know who to believe right now...

April 27th

Henry's teaching is getting worse and worse, and so are his attitudes and behaviours, particularly towards our girls.

He's started slut shaming.

I mean, he did do this a little bit before, but never like this. And I've noticed it's become worse since Lorelei started leading. That's weird isn't it, seeing as she's a woman?

Henry's called Yvanne a slut a couple of times, and gossiped about her and some of the other girls to me.

What is going on?

April 29th

I was out with Lorelei, Henry and some others, when Lorelei started accusing Yvanne and her sister Louise of deliberately choosing to wear revealing tops.

I said, "That's not true, they wear other tops underneath."

And Henry said, "Yeah, really tight ones."

Something is just really off here, and I don't know exactly what, and I don't know what to do about it.

May 4th

The slut shaming is getting worse. Henry keeps targeting Yvanne, gossiping about her clothing choices and her obvious desire for a boyfriend, putting her down by insinuating that she's a slut. He's even gone so far as to warn the boys against her, in case she tempts them.

While I concede that Yvanne is flirtatious, there are better ways to deal with her behaviour, like talking to her in person, privately, so that we don't embarrass her, and so that we can give her some helpful correction.

I suggested to Henry that I have a talk with her, and he said no. Then I asked if Alison, a prior leader, could do it. He said no again. Why doesn't he want us to actually help her?

May 17th

I have been hanging out with the girls from youth group for years now, outside of official youth activities, because I'm friends with them all. That includes some of our younger girls. This has never been a problem before, but now Henry is suddenly trying to discourage me from hanging out with the younger girls, including two of my best friends. He's also trying to discourage the same girls from hanging out with any of us female leaders, even though we've all been friends for years.

May 20th

Lindy's also been trying to discourage me from hanging out with the younger girls, even though they are my friends. I don't know what the problem is. When I tried to ask why, Lindy hinted that she's worried about them gossiping to me about Henry.

Look, fair call to be concerned about gossip. It's become a real problem within this youth group. So I explained to them both that I have told the girls I won't engage in gossip, but I'm still here for them. All the girls accepted that. And I have noticed them complaining about Henry less, since.

But Lindy and Henry don't seem to want to accept this, even though I told them how I've handled the situation.

May 26th

Henry has begun complaining and gossiping about our girls in front of the other leaders. Why does he never gossip about the boys? Why is he targeting the girls?

Once, he'd just finished complaining about how sexual some of our girls allegedly are; then turned straight to me and Renee and asked us to do a girls' talk on healthy sexuality, that very night. With no preparation time. I asked if we could do it next week so we'd have time to prepare, and he said no, he wanted us to do it now.

He gave us ten minutes to prepare before throwing us in the deep end.

May 30th

Henry and Lorelei split up, then got back together. Their relationship has been really volatile. She gossips to him about everyone in the youth group, tries to turn him against us. He told me she once tried to say that he could only trust her.

CHAPTER 24

False Accusations

June 1st

At youth group tonight, Jacinta turned up in a gorgeous leopard print dress with her youth group jumper over the top. She showed some of us girls her dress, which was a bit low cut, but she was going clubbing afterwards, so I didn't see a problem. I mean, she'd deliberately covered up for youth group, because that dress was appropriate for the nightclub but not for youth group. And she'd only shown the girls her dress, not the boys.

Henry and Miles went on and on about her clothing, calling her a slut and bringing up times they'd seen her in "provocative" clothing.

Then some of the other girls started gossiping about Jacinta too, because they heard Henry and Miles do it.

June 5th

Tonight after youth group, Henry drove me and Miles round to Mic's house, ostensibly to check on him and his friends, because he had a party instead of coming to youth group.

When we neared the house, we saw a whole bunch of young girls wearing short skirts, talking and drinking outside on the veranda. Henry said, "Little sluts," then drove off.

We did not actually check on anyone. We didn't even get out of the car! Henry simply used, "let's check on them," as an excuse to slut shame more young girls.

I was so shocked by his behaviour; I began blabbering on about how I know not to wear skirts that short and not to drink, as though trying to prove myself as good enough for him.

Why did I even feel the need to defend myself?

June 6th

Jacinta confided in me that she had been in an abusive relationship when she was only fourteen. She went out with a much older man, and he made her do his housework whenever she went over to his place.

Then he started demanding sex, which escalated until he raped her annually. She has an injury from this, making it painful for her to go to the toilet.

I cried for her and prayed for her. I can't believe she had to go through that. I asked her if she needs to see a counsellor.

June 14th

Henry called Jacinta a slut at youth group, in front of everyone, loud enough for us all to hear.

He called a rape victim a slut. I feel sick.

June 21st

Oh this is awful. I'm not sure what to do. I am glad they came to me though. Good call. Now we can do something about it.

Two youth-group girls came to me, and quietly told me that Jacinta had come to them in tears, saying that she'd been sexually assaulted at a night club.

I told them they had done the right thing in telling me, and explained that I had to tell Henry, because I'm supposed to tell the head leader about serious cases so he can tell the police. They agreed.

Later, I had a conversation with Jacinta, and she was crying as she told me what happened. I told her she needs to report him to the police. She said she's not sure if she wants to and I told her to think about it.

I did tell Henry, and my parents. I've asked Mum and Dad to pray.

About the only other thing I can think of to do, apart from praying, is to offer to go with her to the police, if she decides to go ahead with it.

I feel sick...

June 24th

I spoke to Jacinta and she asked if I could come with her to make a police report. I said, "Yes. I was actually just about to suggest that."

June 27th

I had a meeting with Henry and Lindy about Jacinta, and I asked Henry if he'd reported it to the police yet. He said he didn't want to. I asked him why, and he said he thought she'd made it up for attention, or if it were true, that it hadn't really been that bad.

He's meant to tell the police. There are mandatory reporting laws.

Then they told me they had a meeting with her, where they tried to talk her out of going to the police, because they thought it would be a waste of police time.

Shocked, I said I'd agreed to go to the report with her.

They talked me out of going with her, reiterating that they thought she'd made it up, saying they didn't want her to report it, and saying I shouldn't be that worried about her.

When I questioned why they thought that, they said I cared, "too much about the kids," and the reason I cared was really that, "I hadn't dealt with my own problems," and that me, "caring too much," meant I wasn't doing well as a leader because, "what the kids really need is firmer discipline and not someone to be their spiritual big sister!" They made the bit about, "worrying too much," sound like an accusation, as though me caring for them was somehow selfish, or a sin of some kind. It was so confusing.

Nothing I try doing to improve things seems to work. I've tried prayer, fasting, talking straight to Henry about what I think he's done wrong, asking him questions about what the purpose of his behaviour is, challenging him and just submitting to him. Nothing's working. This is awful. I feel wretched.

June 30th

I have decided to take a break from leading. I just cannot sit under Henry any longer. I don't want to bring my anger at Henry to youth group, and risk letting the kids know what's really going on, or venting my anger at Henry to them. I believe I've made the right decision. Mum and Dad agree.

July 7th

One week's break and I am already feeling a bit better. Dad says I should take a break from regular church for a while too, and come with him to his smaller church instead. Good idea. They are so nice at that church, and the old people look after me like I'm their granddaughter. Might be just what I need.

July 14th

I've been thinking about what Henry and Lindy were saying about me being too caring, and too much of a big sister. I talked to Mum and Dad about it, and I can see now how wrong it is.

Being spiritual family is Biblical. Why do you think Paul calls his congregations, "brothers and sisters in Christ?"

Our girls need a spiritual big sister to go into bat for them, to protect and care for them. The fact that they trust me enough to ask me for support during hard times is evidence of this, not to mention that some of them say they want to be like me. I suggest that me being a big sister to them is working. Perhaps Henry just doesn't like that he's losing his control over them through me being their spiritual big sister?

Henry also said that I had to stop trying to help Jacinta because of my own issues. I don't believe someone having their own issues should disqualify them from helping others. If we all waited until we were completely healed to help others, no one would ever get help.

July 17th

I found out that Jacinta got talked out of reporting to the police. Henry made her think it was her, "promiscuity and provocativeness," that were to blame. So she didn't get the help she needed.

August 15th
I went back to youth group last night. I have talked a few things through with Henry and he's even apologised for some things. This is a good start.

CHAPTER 25

A Prophet's Calling
Called into Question

August 20th

Henry has been saying that all of us youth leaders are pastors, over and over. He says he's trying to encourage us, but I don't see it that way. From where I stand, it seems more like he's trying to control us.

We can't all fit into that box. We don't all have that gift.

Maybe I should talk to him about this.

August 24th

When Henry said, "You are all pastors," tonight, he said it as though he wasn't giving us an option to be anything else. I didn't think this was right, so after the meeting, I talked to him privately about it.

I told him he needs to stop saying this because we don't all have that gifting. I explained that him saying it over and over is putting a lot of pressure on us to conform, and making some of us feel like we can't be who we truly are, nor use our actual spiritual gifts. I said he needs to stop labelling us, because this label, "pastor" might cause him to miss seeing what gifts we actually have, which may in turn cause us not to function properly as a group.

"A body doesn't have just one part. Each part has its own function, and each part is just as important as the others. We can't all be pastors. How would we then function as a body?"

He asked what other gifts I thought we might have, so I started with me, saying, "Well, I'm a prophet."

"What other gifts do the others have then?"

I told him I didn't know about everyone's, but I had observed that Renee has a gift of encouragement, and that she brings joy into a room, and that I thought Miles might have a gift of prayer.

He growled, "How would you know? What makes you think you're a prophet?"

Why are you so angry Henry?

August 25th

Henry rang me and demanded I meet him and Lindy at a café to talk about what I'd told him.

When we met, they told me I have a root of pride because I said I'm a prophet.

I asked why and they went on about us having to be careful of prophecy because there are false prophets, and that real prophets don't tell people what they are, and that I'd told Henry I'm a prophet with pride on my face.

When I tried to explain why I know I have a prophetic gifting, they shut me down again, and manipulated me into apologising to them for being prideful. They should have been the ones to apologise to me. Why did I come back?

I know why. To try and protect the kids from them. That's why.

August 27th

I talked to Dad about what Henry and Lindy said and Dad said they were completely out of line.

I asked Dad if I am prideful and he said no! He said, "Jules, you're really generous and you own up to your wrongdoings. Prideful people don't act like that."

Then he said it's not prideful to know who you are in Christ.

He reminded me of all the times I have operated as a prophet, and helped me remember that I've been doing this since I was five.

He said, "You didn't ask for the ability to see spirits, or for your gift of dreams. In fact, sometimes you wish it would stop, am I right?"

I answered yes and he prayed for me; that I would not let their accusations come against me, that God would tear them off me and use me for his good, despite what those accusers have been saying.

"You use your gifts anyway Jules. God needs you. Don't worry about them."

September 7th

We had a leaders' prayer session together, and Henry asked if anyone wanted to receive certain spiritual gifts from the Lord. He mentioned some specific gifts, including the gift of spiritual sight. I said that I wanted to see, so Henry prayed for me to receive the gift of sight. I reckon he knew I meant an increase in sight, because I've told him before that I can already see.

Anyway, he wanted to test if his prayer for me worked, so he got Kevin to come forward, and asked me what evil spirits I could see in him. I didn't think this was right. I was worried about it being humiliating for Kevin, but I didn't voice this because I didn't think Henry was going to let me say no.

So Kevin stood in front of me, and I looked at him and saw a spirit of doubt start manifesting, followed by a spirit of lust.

As I was watching, the spirit of lust used Kevin's eyes to look me up and down, then it sexually propositioned me by using telepathy.

I said, "You're not supposed to be there," and started crying. I had to leave the room.

I was also mad that these two demons were in one of my friends. I wanted them gone. I was sad for Kevin's suffering.

After a few minutes, Henry came in to where I was, asked me why I'd reacted like that. I told him what the demon of lust had done, and he said, "Ok, but you shouldn't have gotten so emotional."

He told me off for my reaction, then said he didn't think God should have given me the gift of sight, because I couldn't handle it.

Who are you to tell God what gifts he can and can't give others?

You don't get to control other people's reactions, and you don't get to plan what happens in the supernatural. You don't have that much power. A demon isn't going to behave because you planned on it not manifesting quite so much when you wrongfully decided to use your friend as an example. And a young woman forced to bear witness to these demons tormenting her friend, then being sexually harassed by one of those demons isn't going to be happy about it. Are you crazy?

September 15th

So I had another meeting with Henry, this time about something I had actually done wrong. I accidentally sent a private message to Callie, when it was meant to go to Lorelei. When he told me what happened, I said I was so sorry, and explained that I'd meant to send it to Lorelei. He said he knew I wouldn't have done it on purpose, so at least he still has some faith in me.

I am so embarrassed.

Henry just told me to be more careful about what messages I send to whom, and he said he'd talk to Callie about it. He wasn't mad at me this time. A nice change.

September 20th

A weird thing happened after Callie's party. Lorelei started saying there was something spiritually wrong with Henry. I prayed with her, because I also sense that something is going to go quite wrong very soon. Then I drove home, trusting that God would do his work and that I could now just focus on getting a good sleep.

When I got home, Lorelei kept messaging me, asking me to meet with her and Nicholas to report Henry, because she said he has a demon in him.

Eventually, I told Lorelei to stop texting me because I was going to sleep. I wish she'd stop hassling me! Sometimes she reminds me of Phil.

September 21st

After church, Henry approached me and told me he knew Lorelei and I were planning on reporting him, and that he didn't have a demon. I said, "I know. I knew it wasn't true. I told her I wasn't going with her. But she kept texting me last night to try and get me to come."

Henry rolled his eyes, said she was like that. Then he said, "I just wanted to get that clear between us. We've only just started making things right, and I don't want us to go backwards. And if Lorelei says the proof of me having a demon is that my eyes are watery, it's not true. I have hay fever. She's only doing this to get back at me because I disciplined her about something."

I said I knew that none of it was true and we shook hands. I'm finally starting to trust him again.

September 30th

Lindy is so weird! She doesn't want me to preach, even though Henry said I could, and she told me I shouldn't pray for the boy I like because my feelings for him will get in the way of my prayers. Then she said she didn't pray for husband because she has feelings for him.

I really don't think caring for someone disqualifies you from praying for them. In fact, some of my most powerful prayers have been for those I care most about.

October 3rd

Lorelei has gone. Now we have to repair the damage. I don't think it's completely fixable. Our youth group is broken. I hope we can salvage something, but I don't think there's a lot left to salvage.

November 10th

Henry is leaving. He has a new job. I wish him well.

He apologised for a few more things, and although it still irks me that some things he just can't seem to take responsibility for, it also gives me hope, because he has continued to take responsibility for a lot of the things that happened.

It seems like something can be salvaged from this wreck. Our friendship.

December 2nd
We had a leaver's dinner for Henry. He gave a speech, then he publicly honoured me, saying how faithful I am. He even publicly admitted to doing wrong by me; said he is so glad that through it all, we remained friends.

Thank you, Lord! Thank you, Henry!

How good is God, to bring healing from ashes, joy from grief, to restore us to a place of grace, where there had been condemnation. Praise the Lord!

CHAPTER 26

The Birth of the Monthly Gathering

In the midst of this difficult season, Dad, Mum and I travelled up to Launceston for a conference.

During the worship, I was dancing at the back of the room with Dad, when one of the leaders came and asked if I could dance up the front. I was nervous and unsure, because I'd just recently been accused of pridefulness for talking about my gifts. But the leadership wanted me to do it, so eventually, I consented. Although I was nervous, I knew I had to be obedient.

I was trying to dance gracefully with fluid movements, and it wasn't working. That is, until I followed God and just went wild. I realised that he wanted me to dance like a warrior, not like the "nice Christian girl." So I stared pushing my hands out in front of my body, kicking, twirling and punching, like dance fighting. Like kickboxing.

As I continued to follow God, something broke in the spirit, and I really let loose! The dance fighting went up a notch, and became more fierce, but also more fluid and graceful, like a warrior in battle.

After a while, the leadership asked a young man to wave his banners along with my movements. So he and I worked together, changing the atmosphere with our praise. It was awesome.

In the midst of being falsely accused of pridefulness by my own leaders, another leadership team asked me to dance in front of the whole church, restoring me to a place of honour.

It was like God was saying, "There is nothing wrong with you, Jules. I can still use you, even when others are reluctant to."

God used me a lot during this season. I was invited to do some teaching for a worship conference about the use of banners. I was kind of scared to say yes, because I was worried about what Lindy would think. But I did it anyway. One of the men there said he really enjoyed my teaching. God could use me. He didn't need me to fit into anyone's mould. He just needed me to be me.

He made me a warrior, and a warrior I shall be. He needs his warrior princess to be herself.

A New Job

In July 2007, I got a permanent part time position at Fabulous Café. Hank made a special position just for me. It was a great job. It stretched me, taught me new skills, and helped me grow. Hank was an excellent boss, and a caring person, and Holly was a great supervisor. She trained me well. Under her, I learned how to supervise others.

Fabulous was a pumping little café; a place where the locals gathered. Families came for pasta nights, groups of ladies met for lunch, couples celebrated their anniversaries and children had their birthday parties. It was a great spot for a catch up.

That job was like a promotion from God. I'd gone from being the takeaway assistant at Renaissance Café, only working a few hours a week, to being the assistant supervisor at Fabulous, and doing twenty-plus hours per week. Interestingly, it was while I worked there that the monthly gatherings took off. I was simultaneously stepping up at work and in spirit.

God always works for our good, and always within his timing, even when we don't realise it.

A Difficult Year

I did have one very difficult year while working at Fabulous. For starters, I severely hurt my back dancing. I had to lie on heat packs several times daily, and I had to get up in the middle of the night to walk around. If I stayed too long in the one position, my back seized up and I couldn't move.

After this, our family friend Toby was travelling down the highway one winter morning when he skidded on ice and collided with another car coming the other way. Amazingly, Toby had no injuries, but the other driver died. He was pretty cut up about that, and had to have some counselling.

Then Grandpa died, and that hit me like a ton of bricks. I'd been meaning to go up to NSW to visit him and Grandma, because I knew he was sick. But he died before I could get there. I didn't just lose my Grandpa; I lost my art mentor and a friend. Grandpa was such a strong, funny, compassionate character, and a natural leader. People looked up to him wherever he went. We were all sad when he passed.

A few months after Grandpa's death, Candace was driving along Cliff Top Road, which has a steep drop to a creek on one side. Candace moved over to accommodate a large truck coming the other way, but she moved over too far. The car tumbled ten metres down the cliff, into the creek. Miraculously, Candace and her friend, Elisa, were not seriously hurt, but the car was a wreck, all crumpled up, glass smashed.

Immediately after the impact, Elisa was too terrified to move, crying, shaking and unable to work out how to get out of the car. Candace kept a level head, and was able to coax Elisa out the door and guide her as they scrambled up the cliff.

About halfway up, Candace herself began crying uncontrollably and screaming. Elisa stopped freaking out and became calm right at that moment, so she was able to help Candace climb the rest of the way up the cliff. God knew they needed each other.

When they made it to the top, they sat down and called their mothers and the ambulance. While they were waiting for the ambulance to arrive, a man appeared, sat with them, and comforted them. When the ambulance arrived, he vanished. I still think he was an angel.

Winds of Change

One Sunday at church, we had a special arts day. Some artists, including me, were invited to paint a representation of a scripture verse from Genesis chapter one, and the musicians played corresponding music. We all assembled out the front of the sanctuary, canvases, paints and instruments at the ready. When Nicholas gave the word, the artists began painting.

I'd been given the verse about the sea separating from the sky, so I painted a skyscape with billowing clouds rising up from the sea.

When our time was up, Nicholas read the verses out, one by one, pausing after each verse so that the artist with the corresponding artwork could unveil it. Then, while the artists showed their work, the corresponding musicians played their music. I was paired with Bessy. She played a beautiful, slow melody on her tenor saxophone, which paired beautifully with my painting. It was wonderful to do worship differently, for a change.

I began attending a small church in Hobart during this season, the Church of the Living Word (CLW). Dad gave many sermons for them. He explained the prophetic in a creative and intelligent way; a way that even beginners could understand. CLW was a welcome break for me while I was having issues with Henry and Lorelei; a respite from the rumours and stress, and a balm to my wounded soul.

Alicia used to run beautiful worship evenings there once a month. She'd set up the hall with lights dimmed and soft music playing. She'd often bring anointing oil. The smell of it wafted through the doorway as you entered. The atmosphere was so peaceful and calming; it was like Jesus was washing you clean with a bar of anointing oil soap. So beautiful. Sometimes we'd just sit and soak, sometimes we got up to dance, sometimes we used banners. Those evenings were special.

In 2007, Mum and Dad ran a seminar about the Winds of Change. They spoke about their vision, and Mum brought her painting. While Dad was declaring the winds of change, a wind suddenly blew the door shut. Dad said, "It's here!"

Monthly Gathering

On the way home from a day trip one day, Candace said, "Dad, you have to start a once-a-month, all-purpose church, so me and my friends can come." She went on about it all the way home. It was a prophecy that came into fruition in 2008 when we started hosting a monthly gathering.

A small group of us gathered to pray and listen to the Lord. We brought our instruments and played. We often spontaneously broke into worship. We declared things in the Spirit, spoke in tongues and prophesied.

One session, while Dad was playing his drum, I heard words in my head. It was like the drum was speaking. It was saying, "We've won. We've won. The battle we have won," over and over, each word coming forth on Dad's drumbeats. I shared this with the others and someone confirmed it. They said it sounded like the passage in 1 Corinthians about discerning tongues. Jim said, "She interpreted the tongue of the drum." It was amazing, and completely unexpected.

We had a few sessions at the CLW premises before moving the gathering to our house. People gathered in our lounge room each month, and within three months, we'd grown from six members to twenty.

People came from all over the state. It was amazing how God brought exactly the right people each time, and used them to transact whatever was needed for the night.

The gathering ran for ten years. When it started, I don't think anyone was expecting it to go for that long. Actually, to start with we didn't know what we were doing, we were just following God.

At one gathering Dad shared about the use of lamentations in prayer. During the prayer time, the women started to wail. A real grief welled up in us. Grief for young girls who had been groomed and harmed by predatory men. We just wept! It came out as deep, guttural moans of grief, exasperation and despair.

The grief started with the oldest woman, then it continued down the generational line until it got down to the youngest woman present – me. It was like we were expressing the grieved father heart of God for his traumatised daughters.

After the meeting, one of the elders made a point of thanking me for my prayers, for my wailing. This helped me recover my confidence in intercession, confidence I'd lost after being told by Henry that showing emotion in prayer was a sign of weakness. It was so good to have this lie uncovered.

There is nothing wrong with using emotion in prayer. When you really intercede for people from your heart, you feel their pain as your own. You carry a burden for them until it is released back to God. Wailing, weeping, crying and moaning in prayer are Biblical. That's why the Bible says the Spirit cries out for us with moans that words cannot express *(Romans 8:26)*. When you express this type of moaning and weeping in prayer, you are really expressing God's heart for the persons you are praying for. It's necessary, and how intercession works.

It is not a sign of weakness; it's a sign of God's inexpressible words, through raw love. Many mountains are moved, many lives changed, through deep intercession like this. We need to stop labelling it as weak, bad, wrong or even crazy. It isn't any of those things.

Once again, God broke down the lies I'd been told about myself and my gifts. He made it clear that he certainly could, and would, use his warrior princess for good.

CHAPTER 27

The Gatherings Give Us a Voice

Many of us who attended the gatherings had been silenced. We'd been told we weren't good enough; that God couldn't use us because we didn't fit the "good Christian" mould. Many of us had even been told not to talk about our traumas; that doing so meant we were weak and disobedient for "not forgiving" the perpetrators. A number of us had even been blamed for the bad things done to us.

The gatherings were a safe space where we were allowed to talk. We could begin to express ourselves, share our gifts without judgement or criticism, and ask questions about God without immediately being shushed or shamed. It was a place we could heal, grow, and begin to breathe.

During this time, Dad met a lovely Aboriginal woman named Gloria, and she came to some of the gatherings.

One gathering, God asked me to prophesy over Gloria. I had a Jewish coin, a flag of different colours and some Aboriginal clapping sticks. Using these items, I prayed something about the Jewish culture connecting to the Australian Aboriginal culture, and for Gloria's heart for this. When I'd finished, Dad started laughing. He said, "She has no idea!"

He told me that Gloria had just discovered she has Jewish heritage, and that she'd been praying about this very connection earlier that day. It was amazing!

After about a year, we moved the gathering to Toby and Ruth's lovely old farmhouse. Inside, everything was light and airy. They had a lovely big garden with multi coloured roses growing in beds along the fence line, and tall shade trees growing in a line next to the entrance archway; their branches hanging gracefully over the front porch.

At their place, it was like we were sort of covered and protected. We were hidden from view, so that we could practice using our spiritual gifts. Even the location of the house and the way the garden was set out reflected this; tucked into a little valley, hidden behind a wall of beautiful trees.

People used to bring all sorts of things to those meetings. We ended up with so much stuff; Dad had to start telling us to display our things on the coffee table. He called it THE TABLE. "Place your things on the table," became a spiritual phrase. How extraordinary that such ordinary words should become so significant.

People brought jewels, stones, feathers, boxes, books, paintings, newspaper clippings, pens with words printed on them, ornaments, sculptures, weather instruments, strange musical instruments, pictures, photos, articles and poems. We brought anything we thought was significant, anything we felt God was using to speak to us. We were all given time to explain the significance of our treasures.

It was amazing how God used our treasured objects. Often, all the different things matched up. There was always a theme, without any planning.

After a few months of getting used to this, the groups' artists began bringing their artworks, and explaining their meaning and spiritual significance to the group. This was really important to us, because it was a chance to finally be given a space to speak our language, and to show how God was using our gifts; gifts that had so often before been rejected, misunderstood, minimised and misused.

Sometimes I brought my silk paintings and explained their significance. One night, I brought one named, "Ship of Dreams;" a whimsical work symbolising the arrival of the harvest wind and what it brings.

There's an old-fashioned sailing ship in the centre, its sails billowing in the wind, and a figurehead in the shape of a lion, symbolising the Lion of Judah. A mermaid is jumping up in excitement to meet the ship, in order to greet the Lion. Storm clouds are rushing across the sky, bringing fruits with them; fruits that fall into open sacks on the ship's deck, symbolising the work of the harvest.

When I unveiled it to the gathering, Dad called out, "It's here!" They'd been talking about the arrival of the harvest wind only a few days ago.

Rhonda often brought her artwork, too. I remember the time she brought a little quilted banner, with a background of muted browns, purples and oranges, featuring three silver trumpets pointing out into the atmosphere, proclaiming things and making a noise. She used it to explain how it was time for the trumpets to sound.

That same night, Eliora brought her actual silver trumpets and placed them on the table next to Rhonda's artwork. She played them later that night; another example of God putting all the pieces of the jigsaw puzzle together.

Rhonda also brought a handmade scroll that night. When she opened it up, Dad prayed that people would no longer devalue her work. What Dad proclaimed over Rhonda affirmed something in all the artists in the room – our work was important, our work was necessary for God's Kingdom, our work proclaimed things in the spirit and made changes to atmospheres, people and places. Where we had been dishonoured, Dad made a point of restoring honour to us.

Dad's words encouraged me to keep making, even if I wasn't selling much. I learned that some of my artworks just needed to be made, so that their message could be seen and proclaimed. God told me to just keep making what he put on my heart; if I was obedient, he'd provide payment for my work.

I have some great memories of social times with the gathering folk, too. Once, we had a New Year's Eve party at Toby and Ruth's. We had dinner by candlelight and played games. Then Josie and her sisters played piano and we had a sing along. When the fireworks started, we all went out onto the porch to watch.

The fireworks were beautiful, but the natural light show was better! Right at that moment, huge storm clouds gathered around Hobart. Lightning flashed and lit up the sky, turning the clouds purple and gold. The fireworks just couldn't compete with God's glory.

"Anything you can do, I can do better," sang Ruth.

The gatherings were like a class for learning to feel accepted, loved and whole again, and for learning to use our gifts. We all grew in confidence.

After five years, we moved the meetings to Marigold and Renee's place, and there we learned to use our gifts before visitors from all over the world, and we learned how to back ourselves and our prophetic words. This wasn't prophecy 101 anymore. It was now the advanced course, and we had to learn to stay in the truth of who we were, to stay calm even when we failed or were given correction. No more reading from the script, now it was the real thing, and we had to learn to accept ourselves, instead of expecting others to do it for us.

CHAPTER 28

Welcome to the Positive Outlook

We had our first meeting at Marigold and Renee's in mid-2014, after I had married my husband, Timothy, and when our son Bree was about nine months old. The location shift was significant. Marigold and René live in Paraclete Street, paraclete meaning one called alongside as advocate and helper. One member was inspired to say, "Welcome to the positive outlook," while gesturing out the window. Marigold and René have a stunning view of Hobart, so her comment was quite apt.

When I thought about it, I realised that everything about Marigold and Renee's home is positive. Even their colour choices are positive; bright blue, yellow and white, and everything is bright, airy and open. That's what Marigold and René are like too; bright, airy and open. Marigold has a real gift of hospitality. Every time you go to her house, even just for a spontaneous visit, she goes out of her way to serve you.

Their house really did feel like the right place for the unfolding of the positive outlook.

During this season, more and more people began bringing weather instruments and unusual musical instruments.

One night, Toby brought his ship's clock and compass. When he talked about his nautical items, I felt something in my spirit. That same night, someone else brought a model of an old sailing ship, another person brought a drawing of a ship, while still another brought a hand drawn, nautical map. Together we explored the idea of going into uncharted territory.

Discussions about finding our way into the new things God had for us, and navigating into God's truth, continued for about three months. Nautical and coastal objects kept showing up during this season.

Dad's friend Paul told us about his time travelling around the world on various missions. He told us the Christians in Scandinavia had previously been very rigid and strict in their adherence to religious traditions, and that stopped the flow of the spirit. He and his team prayed for them to be set free from these man-made constraints, and the Holy Spirit began to fall on people during their meetings. Suddenly, they were free to hear from God, respond to the Holy Spirit, and move in freedom. After Paul's testimony, we prayed for an increase in spiritual freedom in Tasmania.

I so enjoyed all the unusual musical instruments that turned up during this time, and hearing their sounds. Apart from Paul's conch shell, we had my harp, Eliora's trumpets, a serpentine, a washboard, a blue grass bottle cap shaker, violins, tambourines, rain makers and various drums, including Congas, bodrahns, djembes, Dad's handmade drum and other hand drums from various nations. One night Dad was proclaiming something about the new sound, when he picked up Bree's castanets and used them to pray prophetically over someone. We talked about making a new sound a lot, and we worked hard on sending it forth. We made so much noise, I'm sure the angels joined in.

Spiritual Waste Systems

One night, Allora shared about her recent mission trip to Cambodia. She said the villagers she worked with built her a private toilet block, because they wanted to honour her. She told them that they didn't need to do that, but they insisted.

Allora said she and her teammates had been praying for the release of spiritual waste on the trip, and she commented on how interesting it was that they wanted to build her a personal toilet block at that time.

Afterwards, Mum talked about getting rid of spiritual waste. Then I shared my insight on how pastors are like waste systems in the body of Christ, because they flush out the excrement. Waste systems are important. If your bodily waste system isn't working well, your whole body gets sick with toxicity. Likewise, if the churches' waste system isn't working properly, the body of Christ will also get sick with toxicity.

Then Mum said, "We need to build spiritual toilets then, and have signs marking out where they are, because some people in the body of Christ don't know where they can go to get rid of their spiritual waste."

We all said amen. We didn't want anyone else to get sick from holding in their waste for too long.

Afterwards, when Dad got us all to enter into worship, he asked Billie to blow one of Eliora's trumpets, while he blew another. Dad can actually play a bit, so he made a calling sound. But Billie was having trouble, so when she blew hers, it sounded like a fart.

Dad said, "I'll make the call sound, you make the fart sound." It was funny and quirky, but it worked, because farts are a form of waste. It fit the evening's theme perfectly.

We finished the night by praying for the church to be able to get rid of her spiritual waste.

More Interactions with our Aboriginal Sisters

One evening, an Aboriginal woman named Dianne came to join the gathering. Dianne started talking about how she wanted reconciliation between her people and white Australians. She began weeping, so some of us women gathered around her to pray for her and her people.

I felt to pray that it be the Celts who be the first to apologise for what white settlers had done to her people. Interestingly, all of us gathered around her had Celtic heritage. Then I said that Germanic peoples also needed to apologise to Australian Aboriginal and Torres Strait Islander peoples for their treatment of them. When I said that, Eliora, who is German, came to join in. Then Savannah said she has Germanic heritage too.

Marigold wept as she told Dianne that she also knew the pain of racial rejection. She explained how her family had moved to Australia from Poland when she was a child, and what it was like to live in a new country. She didn't know much English, and she was teased by the other children for not being "Australian." She said she knew the pain of racism too, and she wept to say sorry to this woman on behalf of her people, (Polish people and other Eastern Europeans), for treating Aboriginal Australians so badly.

Then Dianne asked our forgiveness for the way some of the Aboriginal people retaliated, by killing some white settlers. What love and humility she showed. To apologise for any retaliation done by Aboriginal Australians towards white settlers at all, when we were the ones who did the most harm, far more harm than her people have ever done to us.

We hugged her one by one. We all cried.

I had recently finished a silk banner about saying sorry to Aboriginal Australians and convicts for our treatment of them. It has a map of Tasmania patch worked onto it, in patterned, Aboriginal fabric, and a picture of Trugannini and King Billy sewn onto the map. Concentric circles radiate out from trouble spots on the map, as a way of showing that those places need focused prayer for healing and change. At the top of the painting is an angel blowing a silver trumpet, heralding in change. And in the centre of the map, I sewed a heart shaped jewel, showing Father God's heart of love for Tasmania, and how he wants to bring healing to us.

I made a real connection with Dianne, so I gave her this artwork. She ministers in prisons in the NT, and I asked her to use it in her ministry.

It was an amazing night of heartfelt love and care for each other, and of a genuine desire for reconciliation, displayed through raw, heartfelt apologies to each other for past generational sins. I've never before seen such a real, genuine desire for change.

Bombs Away and the Welcome Home Party

One night at Toby and Ruth's, I felt Timothy and I were meant to bring a bomb. Not an actual bomb, but a spiritual one that would set others free to worship. I wasn't sure what to bring to represent this, so I looked into getting a firework licence, and I researched how to make a cake called an Alaskan Bombe. Neither of these options was going to work. The firework licence was going to take a few weeks to come through, and the Alaskan Bombe was too hard to make.

I ended up bringing a song called, "The Power of One," and Timothy said he might do some dancing. When the time was right, Timothy danced. He span around and around, his arms in the air, his eyes closed, his legs going as fast as a cartoon road runner while his feet tapped out the rhythm. I sometimes wonder how he stays upright!

At the end of the night, Wanda said to him, "You are the bomb! When you dance, you set off a spiritual bomb. You need to do it more often. Do it at home too, especially when there's conflict."

So that's what Timothy has done ever since. And it works. It changes the atmosphere when he dances.

At one gathering at René and Marigold's, Josie and I worked together to bring a party. I brought some helium balloons, and one of them had the words, "Welcome home" printed onto it. I realised this was meant to be a welcome home party; a time to celebrate being welcomed into God's Kingdom, and a time to pray for the lost ones who have not yet been brought into God's family.

We displayed the balloons on the coffee table, so they'd be the first thing people saw as they walked in. The welcome home balloon took pride of place, because I wanted people to read the words and take them in as they got settled for the evening.

We explained why we'd brought a party with us. I talked about us needing to be thankful for where we are; home in God's house, and how we need to welcome the lost back home to Jesus. Josie talked about how parties are filled with joy, and marked with happy rituals, like cake cutting. She said we need to use physical rituals to mark out our feelings of celebration, because it helps us remember why we're celebrating, both now and in the future.

Then she said we need to celebrate being in God's Kingdom more than anything, and I called out, "Welcome Home!" to everyone. Afterwards, we prayed for the lost.

I vividly remember Mavis' baptism. It was held at the beautiful Sparkling Creek, where a series of little cascades tumble joyfully down colourful rocks into a row of cool, deep pools. Mavis was baptised in the bottom pool, under a lovely little waterfall. What a spot for it!

A man named Joseph took the service. His sermon was on the passage in Mark about the woman with the issue of blood.

It was the first time I'd been able to fully grasp this passage. When Jesus called the woman "daughter," and spoke to her gently, he healed her emotional wounds. He took the trauma of being ignored and victim-blamed for her illness from her soul. And he affirmed her with that beloved name.

She'd spent so long being rejected by society for her illness that she became desperate; desperate enough to risk touching a man, and possible further shunning as a result. When she touched Jesus, she was not only given complete physical healing, but emotional healing as well. Incredible.

ACT 4

The Warrior Lives in her Calling

Happy, romantic music builds to a swelling crescendo, and the warrior princess allows herself to fall in love...

CHAPTER 29

How I met my Husband

The Warrior Learns Swing Dancing

At the end of 2007, I looked through the phone book for available dance lessons, and chose swing dancing. Classes were held every Wednesday night. After my first lesson, I decided to come every week.

I had such fun learning to dance. Not only was I learning a new skill, I was also learning to be comfortable in my own body again; to shed the old feelings of shame about the ways I was "allowed" to move my body, and what I was "allowed" to wear.

Every Wednesday night, after lessons, we danced to a live jazz band. Those nights were fantastic. We had great fun asking each other to dance, enjoying the music, drinking and talking. In April that year, a few of us went to a swing exchange in Launceston. The lessons were great, and after dinner, we attended a swing ball, and danced all night to a live band.

June 20ᵗʰ 2008

Tonight I went to a swing exchange with Josie and her sisters. It was so much fun!

I was watching some of the other dancers, when I noticed a young, handsome man, who was very smiley, and a wonderful dancer. I thought to myself, "I need to ask him to dance!"

Halfway through the evening, I had a birthday dance; where the birthday person stands in the middle of a circle, and as the music plays, different people come in to dance with them.

As I was dancing with Ben, the young man I'd noticed earlier cut in to ask me to dance. I was so pleased. I knew he'd dance with me. And he was as good a dancer as he looks.

He introduced himself as Timothy.

June 21ˢᵗ

We had a BBQ dinner at the campsite where we were staying, then got ready for the swing ball, to be held in a local hall. The hall looked fabulous, decked out with blue fairy lights strung from the ceiling, and a montage of red lights covered with red gauzy fabric. Around the walls hung pictures of fire and ice, and the stage was decorated with white paper snowflakes. Everyone looked fabulous in their costumes! Some were dressed as fire, others as ice.

After the ball, there was a fantastic blues after party at the campsite. The was such a great atmosphere. Bluesy, funky music blared from the speakers, the fire was blazing in the hearth, the lights were dimmed, and the organisers were serving hot soup.

The music was so good; we danced for hours.

Later, I sat and talked with Timothy and his friend. I was really impressed when he asked me what I wanted to do with my life, what gives me purpose. Not many people ask that. I told him that I was soon to run a creative women's retreat, to help women know they can be creative and that they are important, because we are all made in God's image.

He seemed genuinely interested in what I had to say. The best part was that he focused on my face the entire time, rather than looking elsewhere, and not really listening at all, like some men do.

June 22nd 2008

I was standing on the balcony after brekkie, when Timothy joined me. I thought he followed me out there, but he said he'd just had a feeling he should come out on to the balcony, and he hadn't even known I was there. It must have been God.

I told him about my family, and how we all get on, and Timothy said, "I don't have that with my family." He told me that his father is an alcoholic, and that he hasn't seen his sister for two years.

I asked if his dad was still drinking and he said his father had been sober eighteen years. "Doesn't that mean he's not an alcoholic anymore?" I asked. Timothy explained that he still called himself an alcoholic, because he couldn't drink a sip, or it might send him back to addiction.

Later in the afternoon, we went to a Hobart pub for some more dancing. I saw Timothy and Ben walk in, so I went to join them. After a while, I got up to stretch, and Ben asked, "Are you wanting someone to dance with?"

I said, "Yes, but I don't know who to ask." He and Timothy looked beat, so I wasn't going to ask them. But then Ben piped up, "You're dancing with Timothy."

So Timothy and I had a few more dances.

I was beginning to like him more and more, so I decided to give him my number. I drew a picture for him and put my number on the back. About half an hour later, he gave me a comic he'd drawn for me, with his number on the back.

June 23rd
I started praying for Timothy's family today; that his father would know he doesn't have to be defined by his addiction, and for him to know that he is a new creation. Then I prayed for his sister to contact the family again.

June 26th
I hope Timothy calls me this week. I've decided I won't call him; I'll let him call me. I'm sick of chasing men and trying to get things to work. If he likes me, he'll call me. End of story. I'm not going to waste my time worrying about it.

July 1st
I'm having a party in a couple of weeks. I wonder if I should invite Timothy. I asked Mum and Dad about it, and Mum said it would be OK, as long as he doesn't stay with us, because none of us know him very well.
That was a good idea.

July 10th
Last week I rang Timothy to invite him down to the party. Today he rang to tell me he's booked flights and accommodation, and I've agreed to pick him up.

July 17th

I picked Timothy up from his hotel, then took him walking around Battery Point and Salamanca. I said, "I'll show you some secret stairs no one knows about," and I took him to Kelly's Steps.

When we got back to my place, Timothy said, "You know, I think those stairs are on my map of Hobart."

When he showed me, I burst out laughing!

Mum and Dad liked Timothy straight away; a good sign.

Mum said, "He's OK Jules, I like him." When I asked her why, she said, "The dog didn't even bark at him."

She was right. The dog did not bark at all. In fact, he wagged his tail. That never happened with Phil. Abbi barked at him every time he came to the door.

July 19th

Today, Jade, Timothy and I went to the Explorer Forest. We saw many varieties of trees, plus the twin rivers flowing into the Explorer. The moss was thick on the native pines and Antarctic beech that were lining the river, and tall swamp gums reached right up, their branches touching the sky. We stood watching the tannin-stained water whoosh past, while listening to the birds twittering in the overhead branches.

I plucked a leaf from a tree, smelled its fragrance and said, "Yeah, it's a myrtle."

Timothy said, "You know what tree it is by the smell?!" He was really impressed!

We had afternoon tea at the café, then Timothy and I shared our first kiss, on the veranda.

At the airport, Timothy told me he was surprised I'd invited Jade. I said that was because I didn't know him well, and it was for safety.

He said, "Oh, I was wondering if that meant you didn't like me romantically, and you were trying to tell me you just want be friends."

I giggled and said, "No, I like you. Wasn't me kissing you a bit of a giveaway?"

July 20th

I was having my prayer time this morning when I felt an intense burden to pray for Timothy's sister. For some reason, it felt important to pray that she be set free from bondage. I don't know what that means, but I couldn't shake the urge to pray for her this way.

July 21st

I still feel that it's really important to pray for Bernice and for her to be liberated from bondage. I still don't know why, but I know it's important, so I continued to pray for her today. This time I again said a prayer that she contact her family again, and that they be reconciled.

July 22nd

I have decided to pray intensely for Bernice for a week. I'll hold her up in prayer every morning.

I'll also keep praying for the family.

July 25th

Timothy rang me, all excited. Bernice has contacted her family again. What an answer to prayer!

July 27th

I rang Timothy, told him I needed to talk to him about our relationship.

I said I don't want to have sex before marriage, and I don't think I can marry a non-Christian. I just wanted to be upfront and honest about things, so that he knows what I expect from him, and where my boundaries are.

I said I can date a non-Christian, but the Bible says not to marry one, and I want to honour that. Then I said it's OK that he's not a Christian right now, and told him it's OK if he feels like he needs to break up with me because of that. I don't want him to feel pressured to be a Christian, but I had to let him know that it has to be on the cards if we get serious. Otherwise, it wouldn't be fair on him.

He said he'd look into it, but he's not promising anything, and I said, "That's OK."

Then he asked exactly what I meant by no sex before marriage. I asked why he asked that and he said he just doesn't want to start doing something he'd normally assume to be fine, and have it upset me.

Oh. He is such a gentleman. He wants to know exactly what I mean, so that he knows exactly where my boundaries are, and doesn't accidentally break them. He doesn't want to hurt me. He wants to know for my sake, not his.

How wonderful!

July 28th

Timothy and I speak regularly on the phone now. We tell jokes and silly stories, and talk about what we've been up to.

We share the same sense of humour. And this time, I don't get any sense that he's faking it, faking liking my jokes to reel me in, like Samson did. He seems to genuinely find me funny.

I don't feel worried about him suddenly getting mad at me either, like I did with Phil. And nor do I get the sense that he's up to something, biding his time until he has me hooked enough to try and coerce me to do sexual things, like Samson did.

I think I've finally found a man I can trust.

August 7th

I haven't heard from Timothy in over a week. I really hope this just means that he's lost his phone or something.

I actually believe that's all it is, because he was so into me before, and he doesn't seem like the kind of person to just not tell me if he's no longer interested. I reckon he'd call me to tell me if that were the case.

I hope I'm right.

I am not going to ring him. I wasted so much time in my other relationships. I refuse to do so this time. If he's genuine, he'll put as much work into it as I do.

August 8th

Timothy rang me. He said he'd lost his phone and was calling from a work phone. He wanted to see me, so we arranged for him to come down next month.

September 8th

I picked Timothy up from the airport, and we had dinner at the wood-fired pizza place, then went out with friends. Mum said it was okay for him to stay at our house this time, because we know him a bit now.

He went home this arvo. I miss him already!

September 16th

I am in Melbourne, visiting Timothy. He's taken four days off work, and he hired a car so he can show me around.

Just before meeting Timothy, I'd asked God for a sign; "Can you please ask the right man for me to buy me a set of seventy-two Derwent pencils in a wooden case for my birthday? Then I will know he's the one you've given me."

We were looking for somewhere to eat when we came across an art shop. I looked in the window and admired the Derwent pencils in their wooden case. Timothy asked what I was looking at, so I told him I'd always wanted a set like that. He replied, "I might be able to buy some for you for your birthday."

I certainly have something to ponder now.

I chose a Thai restaurant, and the waitress seated us at an outdoor table. We were right near the musician.

Timothy pulled a chair out for me, but I didn't realise, so I sat down on the other chair. I kept turning around so I could see the musician.

I said, "I wish I didn't have to keep turning my head around to see."

Timothy replied, "That's why I pulled the chair out for you, so you could sit here and watch the musician more comfortably."

"Sorry," I said. "I thought you were going to sit there."

"No, I was doing it for you. Would you like to sit here?"

I said yes and walked over to the other chair. Then Timothy pulled it out for me again. But I sat down too late and fell on the floor.

We both burst out laughing, and tried again. This time, we managed.

That is the exact moment I allowed myself to fall in love with him. I was already falling for him, but I was guarding my heart, making sure he was trustworthy before giving my heart to him.

My guard fell away in that moment, as I realised I could trust him. He laughed at the funny situation. He laughed with me. He didn't get mad at me for falling over, like Phil would have. This feels like the sign I needed that he most certainly is a good man.

We had a lovely evening; talking, laughing, enjoying the music and sharing delicious Thai dishes. I looked into his sparkling blue eyes and thought, "I like this one. And I am falling in love with him. And I think it's safe to this time."

It's reassuring that everyone around me likes him too. My friends and family have been giving me positive feedback about him. So different to the warnings I had about Samson and Phil.

Thank you, Lord!

CHAPTER 30

The Relationship Grows

Hopeful joyous romantic orchestral music plays in the background, and the warrior princess finds herself finally falling in love with a good man, and finally being truly, respectfully loved in return.

Jules' Diary, September 2008 - July 2009

September 24th 2008

Timothy and I talk on the phone most nights now, often well into the night. We talk about many things, including the Christian faith.

I've given Timothy a New Testament because I think he needs to know about God. Recently, he borrowed a full Bible from the library, and he's begun reading it. I'll keep praying for him.

September 26th

Timothy told me he'd been walking in the city when someone gave him a tract. He asked me, "What's plasm thirty-seven colon three? It was written on a piece of paper I was given about the Bible."

Naturally, Timothy was wondering what a colon was doing in between two numbers. I don't know why we don't explain the way the Bible's chapter and verse system works when we give non-Christians scripture references. We shouldn't just expect them to understand.

I told him that "plasm" was Psalms, and actually pronounced "salms", because it's a Hebrew word with a silent p. Then I explained that the colon represents the word, "verse", and the numbers on either side of it represent the chapter and verse numbers.

"So Psalm 37:3 means the thirty-seventh psalm in the book of Psalms, and verse three of that psalm," I explained.

He said, "Aaah!" Then he got out his borrowed Bible, looked up Psalm 37, and read it. "Trust in the Lord and do good; dwell in the land and enjoy safe pasture".

Yep. He got it.

October 4th
Timothy has begun attending church. Praise the Lord!

October 23rd
I'm in Melbourne for Timothy's swing ball. He paid for half my flights.

We danced to live music, then I watched Timothy perform. Afterwards, we danced until midnight. One of Timothy's friends gave us a lift home, and during the drive, she asked Timothy where I was staying. He said I was staying with him, and he told her he'd given up his bed for me, while he slept on the couch. She said, "That's very chivalrous of you."

It was, too.

November 29th
Timothy asks some cracker questions about Christianity. Sometimes I can answer him, other times I have to say, "I'll just put you onto my Dad."

December 6th
This weekend I went to Bendigo for Timothy's family Christmas do. Timothy and his parents, Allan and Rebecca, met me at the airport.

Christmas lunch was held underneath the terrace at the park. We ate fresh ham and Rebecca's delicious salads, and drank champagne.

After lunch, Timothy introduced me to everyone. It was a bit overwhelming because he has a huge family. I really enjoyed all the family Christmas activities.

As we were saying goodbye, Allan hugged me and said, "I'm glad I met you. He looks happy."

That made me happy too.

Back in Melbourne, we ate ice cream while strolling along the banks of the Yarra. Then, at the airport, Timothy gave me a kiss and said, "You're so beautiful, Jules."

I asked if he meant good looking, and he replied, "Yes, you are that, but I meant you have a beautiful heart. You care about others, where most of my other girlfriends were selfish. You're the first girl I've met who thinks of others."

December 24th
Timothy flew in today. He's spending Christmas with us. After tea, we went for a walk to look at the Christmas lights.

When Timothy was in the bathroom, Candace said, "I'm not inviting my boyfriend to Christmas lunch Jules, it's for family." I replied, "Timothy kind of is like family in a way."

My comment made Mum realise I'm pretty serious about him. I just feel really comfortable with him. There's no abuse and no trying to make it work, it just does. I already know he's the one for me.

As 2009 began, Timothy and I made time to see each other as often as possible. He came to Tasmania and I travelled to Melbourne. Easter found us camping on the east coast of Tasmania.

Easter Saturday, 2009

This morning we went for a walk along the beach. Such a beautiful morning! The clouds were pale violet, and the sun shone through them in shades of pale gold and peach; sunlight sparkling on the clear turquoise waves as they rolled into shore.

We enjoyed climbing the fantastic granite boulders covered in red lichen. Then we went back to the campsite via the lagoon. It was bright blue, and lined with tea trees. Dragonflies skimmed along its surface to find tasty treats, and swallows darted in and out of the trees, swooping low over the water.

After breakfast, we drove south and stopped for a break at Jennesaret Beach. Timothy walked among the boulders while I snorkelled. I saw huge blue groupers and lots of kelp fish darting through the kelp forest.

As I was drying myself, I admired the splendid view of the clear, crystal water, the red lichen-covered rocks, the kelp beds and the little rock pools, all bordered by pure white sand and a clear blue sky.

After looking at the Cape Tourville lighthouse, we leaned against the lookout railing to watch the sunset. The sky turned pale apricot, and the slanting rays of the sun shone through a blanket of clouds, turning them bruised purple. The sun sank towards the horizon, becoming a line of blazing orange.

As we stood there, I noticed two rocks poking up from the sea, not too far from shore. They were made of thick, sedimentary layers, in stripes of bright yellow ochre and burnt orange. The sun shone on them in such a way that they glowed, their bright hues juxtaposing beautifully with the indigo water and their reflections mirroring them perfectly in shiny, golden lines.

Timothy turned to me and said, "I love you, Jules." It was lovely to hear those words, knowing they were genuine.

Easter Sunday, 2009

We drove to Honeymoon Bay, where I snorkelled among the kelp gardens. I was going to swim out further when realised I was really cold. While I was trying to undo my wetsuit, the cold hit me. My vision blurred and I became disoriented. I had to ask Timothy to undo my wetsuit for me, because my fingers had stopped working.

I shook uncontrollably, and I felt really dizzy. Then my vision blurred even more, to the point where I couldn't even see the change rooms though they were literally only ten metres in front of me.

Timothy picked up my clothes and carried them to the change rooms for me, then he helped me get dressed. I put on my trousers, two pairs of thick socks, two tops, a jumper and a vest, but I was still cold.

Timothy led me back to the car and turned the heater on full. He looked after me so well. He even put on a music play list he made for me. On it, he put all the songs we'd been singing to each other that weekend: Yellow Submarine, I Want to Hold your Hand, Octopuses' Garden *and* Happy Together. *It certainly helped me focus on something other than feeling cold. I finally warmed up two hours later.*

He flew home this evening. I'm beginning to find the distance hard.

June 20th
Timothy flew down for my birthday. He presented me with a birthday gift of seventy-two Derwent pencils in a wooden box. Exactly what I'd asked God for.

July 7th
Timothy rang me to say he's thinking of asking his boss if he can work from home. He wants to move to Tasmania, so he can be close to me.

I have mixed feelings about this. I want to be closer geographically to him, but it seems like a big step.

July 14th
Timothy rang to say that his boss has approved him working from home. This is really happening.

July 29th
Timothy's come down to look for houses. I'm sick, so I can't help him. Dad picked him up from the airport.

When he arrived, I was lying in bed with the flu. He entered my room, kneeled down beside my bed and began talking to me. Then he suddenly said, "You look hot."

I said, "Yeah, I think I have a bit of a fever."

"No, I mean, you look beautiful."

"But I'm sick in bed. My hair is dishevelled. How can you think I look beautiful?"

"But you do!"

Strangest compliment I'd ever had! But it's so nice to know he thinks I'm beautiful even when I'm sick. He likes me as I am. He doesn't try to change me.

July 30th

Dad took Timothy into Hobart this morning to look at houses. At lunchtime, Timothy rang to say he'd found a share house in West Hobart. He's organised to move here in September.

CHAPTER 31

Timothy Proposes, and
We Prepare for Marriage

The happy, romantic, orchestral music rises to a crescendo, and the prince finally gets his bride.

Jules' Diary, November 2010 - December 2011

November 16th 2010

Timothy and I have decided to move in together. We've found a house in West Hobart.

Early on, we decided to wait for sex until marriage, so we're honouring that by having separate rooms. He's in the room on the east side of the house and I'm in the room facing west.

We've made a rule that we can't go into each other's bedrooms without permission, and not at night, unless for cleaning, or some other non-romantic activity.

I'm pretty sure this will work. We're both pretty determined, and we're not hormonal teenagers anymore. And we both really want to honour God. So, I reckon we'll be OK.

December 1ˢᵗ

Janelle has moved in with us too. She's got the room that adjoins mine, via a shared door.

Having Janelle here really works as a deterrent for me not to disobey God. If I even wanted to attempt sleeping with Timothy before marriage, I'd have to sneak through Janelle's room to get to his. She'd know. That would be so awkward.

February 4ᵗʰ 2011

Timothy and I were lying on my bed in the sun, cuddling and talking, when I asked Timothy how he was going with dealing with his issues. He said he'd pretty much dealt with them.

Then he turned to me in the sunlight and said, "I love you, Jules. Will you do me the honour of being my wife?"

I said yes immediately, and we shared a celebratory hug.

Later I became upset because his proposal hadn't been what I'd hoped for. The problem was that I had a picture in my head about what proposals should look like, and when Timothy's was different to that, I felt disappointed. I had to hand that over to God, and accept the better, although different, reality. I had to realise that I'd much rather have a tamer proposal and an awesome marriage than a fairy tale proposal and an unhappy marriage. The relationship is more important.

February 14ᵗʰ

Timothy took me to our favourite park for a picnic. He put in so much effort. He brought blueberries, cold meats, cheeses, cherry tomatoes, strawberries, salad, dark chocolate and wine. All my favourites.

Then he took me on a fancy bus tour of Hobart and we ended up at the Botanical Gardens. While we were having afternoon tea, he surprised me with my ring. He got down on one knee and asked me if I would marry him. I said yes and he picked me up and twirled me round. I'm so happy!

I know he already asked and I already said yes, but he knew the big romantic gesture was important to me, so he gave me that too! He's so thoughtful and romantic. I love him!

February 25th

We started pre-marriage counselling today. We talked about dealing with any previous issues so that we don't bring too much baggage into the marriage. The counsellor suggested we both get some separate counselling. I think that's a good idea.

March 20th

We have been having separate counselling sessions so that we can deal with any leftover past issues. Two more sessions each and we're done. I think this will really help us; give us a good, solid grounding for our marriage.

When I told my counsellor about how Samson stuck his hands down my pants, she said, "That is a real violation! You would have said no, before passion took over."

She summed it up exactly!

It's the first time I've been brave enough to see it for what it was: abuse. Hearing her say it like that has allowed me to begin to see that I wasn't to blame.

March 24th

Timothy wants to get baptised before our wedding. He's started doing some baptism studies with Dad and Grandma.

I join in too, because I want to be involved in this important step of Timothy's.

April 5th
 I have been panicking about commitment. Not because I don't want to marry Timothy, but because I'm worried that when I submit to him as my husband, things will change, and I'll suddenly have no rights. I'm worried that he'll turn nasty, like Phil did. What if submission really just means abuse? What do I do then? I'm scared.
 I want to obey God, but I don't know how. Surely Godly submission can't mean "do whatever your husband says". Surely God doesn't want Timothy to abuse or control me.
 I don't think Timothy will actually do that, but I'm scared nonetheless.
 What do I do, God?
 I have decided to study that passage in Ephesians, to see what it's really saying. I have decided that it can't mean that I just lay my rights and personhood down and lose myself when I get married. God wouldn't want it that way. I mean, he made me as I am, so he must want me like this for a reason.

April 9th
 I talked to Timothy about my fears. I told him I can't be the super-subservient wife who does everything for him and gives him whatever he wants. I said, "I can't do that, because God made me a leader and a warrior. I don't want to NOT be who God made me, because I feel like that would dishonour God, and I have to honour him first, above you. Is that going to work? Do you still want to marry me?"

Timothy replied, "Jules! Of course I still want to marry you! I want to marry YOU, not some idea of you. I know you are a warrior and a leader. I know you won't just do whatever I say, because that's not who you are. I want you to give me feedback about my leadership anyway. Your input is important. We're equals."

I am so relieved. I can still be me. I don't have to become someone else to get married. Phew!

April 10th

I have looked up what submit and obey mean in the Hebrew. Obey means listen to and submit simply means pay attention to; refer to (that) authority for guidance. It does not mean do whatever he says.

It sounds to me like I just need to allow Timothy to take the lead, like I do in dancing.

It doesn't mean I don't get a say. It just means that in most circumstances, he makes the final decision. That implies that I will sometimes be called upon to lead, and that my leadership is just as necessary. But in marriage, my leadership is for specific times and seasons, whereas his is for always, so it always goes back to the default setting, where he leads.

*If my leadership is just as important, I can rest in the assurance that I **am** needed, I **am** important, and my job as a wife is not just to be used. The whole idea of the man being the overseer of the family is so that he can protect the woman's power, and help her come to full fruition in Christ. It is not a taking thing, but a giving one.*

I'm getting it.

If I remind myself that Timothy has always let me take the lead when I feel God wants me to, and he's never been territorial about his position as a leader, then I'll be OK.

And if I think of it as a dance, I'll be able to do it.

Thanks for giving me a way to be able to obey you, Lord. And thanks for giving me such a good understanding!

August 14th

I was listening to Amy Grant's "Thy Word," and crying to God about still being afraid of submission.

I told him I can't go through the wedding without him, and he said, "You won't have to. I'll be with you. I will walk you down the aisle too."

*So I'll have Dad and **Dad** with me. I cried in relief and thanks to God. I can do this!*

December 10th

Timothy got baptised today! At Mountain Vista Beach. Nicholas took the service. A small crowd gathered to witness this important occasion. Now he's made fully alive in Christ, and that makes him fully ready to marry me.

CHAPTER 32

Our Wedding

The most beautiful, Heavenly music plays as the Warrior Princess and her handsome Kingdom Knight become one.

On November 19th, 2011, everything was planned and ready to go. Perry was going to marry us at church, then we would have afternoon tea and dancing in the hall, and dinner at Pleasant View Hotel.

My nails were done, (rainbows!) My dress was ready, (so pretty!). The girls had their dresses, the boys had their suits. The catering was taken care of.

Louana and I spent the morning making our bouquets. The next day, Renee decorated the hall before the wedding started.

November 19th[th]
Our wedding day!
I had breakfast and drove to Mum's place to get ready. Timothy and the boys got ready at our house.

The girls helped me get into my outfit. They look beautiful in their dresses. Candace did our hair. She put mine in a pretty up do with twists and braids going into a ponytail. We finished off our makeup and then we were good to go.

We lined up, ready to walk down the aisle. I was so nervous!

My music started playing, (*Thy Word* by Amy Grant,) so Louana started walking, then Breanna, then Candace. Then it was my turn to walk down with Dad and God. I was that nervous, Dad had to remind me to breathe.

Timothy started crying when he saw me, and that got both our mothers going. As I drew closer to Timothy, I began to feel more at ease. By the time Dad handed me over, I was smiling and ready.

I must say Timothy looked very handsome in his top hat and tails.

When it was time to give Timothy his ring, I choked up. There's something really solemn and special about giving a ring, a symbol of forever.

Perry's sermon was on Ecclesiastes 4. For some reason, he emphasised the part about lying together, putting all the emphasis on the innuendo. That set Breanna and Candace off into a giggle loop. Try as they might, they could not stop laughing. In the end, the whole bench was shaking with their silent laughter. Candace was practically wetting herself, trying so hard to stop. It was hilarious!

After the sermon, we signed the register and Perry pronounced us husband and wife. Timothy was waiting for Perry to say, "You may now kiss the bride," but Perry didn't say it fast enough for him, so Timothy leaned in to kiss me before those words were spoken. I kissed him back, then I kissed him again, and everyone laughed and clapped.

I won't go into detail about my first night with my husband, but I will say this. I was ready this time. Even though I didn't know what I was doing, I wasn't scared anymore.

It was lovely. Timothy was even a gentleman in bed. He kept checking I was OK and asking me what I wanted. It was about giving and receiving love, not about our own selfish fulfilment. And that's how it should be.

CHAPTER 33

The Warrior Takes on a Dragon

In 2012, while Timothy and I were on the West Coast for our first wedding anniversary, we were given a strange assignment from the Lord. We went to the town of Tullah, to pray through the town. Soon after arriving, we felt to pray over the local Anglican Church.

As we were standing at the front steps, praying over the church, I got a sense that a wind needed to come through the church and sweep away the cobwebs. Timothy and I prayed this for quite some time, then we saw lots of spider's webs around the cornices of the building – a visual representation of what we'd been praying. We began to pray that the people in the church would be set free to worship in spirit and truth; that they'd no longer be stifled, and that they'd be able to easily share their faith with other people in the area.

After that, we walked to the nearby school and prayed in the adjoining playground. While there, I kept getting a sense that there was an evil dragon spirit watching the children. I looked around the playground, and there under the tree was a horrible dragon statue, all evil eyes and claws, with a menacing watching face.

Why would you put that in a kid's playground?

Timothy and I prayed it would no longer be able to watch the children; that its eyes would be cut out so that it would be made blind.

While we felt this prayer had been effective, I still felt there was more to do around the town. I walked over to the bank of a little stream running through the town and looked into the water. I was asking Holy Spirit what to do next, when I saw two little welcome swallows darting over the creek. I felt to follow them. As I was telling Timothy this, they darted away up the creek.

We followed them all the way up the creek, until it went under the highway. Then we stopped to take stock, and I realised God wanted us to cross the highway to a house and talk to its residents.

We walked tentatively up the driveway, hoping we'd be welcomed. About halfway up the drive, a big dog came bounding out, barking his way towards us. Timothy wondered if it was a sign we'd gone the wrong way, but I knew we were meant to talk to these people.

While we were discussing this, a man came out, saw us and called his dog off. Then he invited us to come and talk with him on his front porch.

He asked us what we were doing, and we explained we were praying through the town. I told him about where we'd already prayed, then asked if there were any other places he thought we should pray over. He told us about Old Tullah – another part of town on the other side of the highway. We didn't even know it existed.

We stopped for lunch, but I couldn't shake the feeling there was another dragon we had to fight, and that it was somewhere in the hills behind Tullah.

We hopped back into the car, ready for a drive. As we were driving along the road, Timothy suddenly felt to stop on the roadside. I didn't want to, because I just wanted to get our spiritual assignment done. By then I was feeling nervous about fighting a dragon.

But Timothy insisted, "There's something on the roadside we need for our task."

I had no idea what we were looking for, so I let Timothy do most of the looking. After about fifteen minutes, he emerged from the scrub with a big, mouldy old stick.

I asked, "What are we going to do with that?"

"It's your staff."

I was dumbfounded. Me? A young girl, use a staff like a real prophet?

I was really nervous to accept it from Timothy because of the conditioning I'd been through as a youth; conditioning that made me think I couldn't possibly be worthy to use the gift of prophecy, much less a staff!

I took a big sigh, "God, I don't want to do this. I don't know *how* to do this! I'm not strong enough. It's a dragon and I'm only a young girl. How am I supposed to conquer it?"

As I stood listening to Father God, those lies slipped gradually away, to be replaced by past memories of how God had moved, and the teachings from the monthly gatherings.

I realised I could do this, because Christ was in me.

"Sorry Lord. I'll do it if you want me to. I suppose when I'm weak, you're strong."

I took a big breath, cried a few nervous tears that were also tears of acceptance, then got back in the car with my staff.

Soon after, I told Timothy we should drive up a small trail that wound up the back of the opposite mountain. I had a feeling the dragon was up there. We drove up that trail as far as we could. Then I got out and listened to God, waited for Him to tell me why we were there.

Even though I didn't get a specific answer, I could sense the dragon's presence.

I told Timothy I wasn't sure what to do, and he said he thought we should continue driving to the dam. We drove back down the track, then continued along the highway till we saw a sign directing us to the dam. We took a right-hand turn, and drove for a while along the lake shore, the mountains obscured from view by the surrounding forest. Then we rounded another corner and crossed a bridge, and the mountain came into view.

When I looked behind me at the mountain, I was dumbfounded. The mountain *was* the dragon – its head the rocky bump at the top of the mountain, it's feet the rounded peninsula jutting into the lake. The rocky "head" had cracks and fissures in it that full-on resembled a face; a menacing scowl on its mouth, and poisonous eyes glaring out at the surrounding landscape.

For a few minutes, we stood in amazement! Then we began to pray.

A torrent of God-given words spilled forth from my mouth, and I was able to take on the dragon. I stood glaring back at it, telling it that it no longer had power over the local area; that it was no longer allowed to rule these people.

"This area belongs to God, and you are not to steal from it him anymore. You are no longer allowed to steal the people's salvation, and you must let go of your power over them, because Jesus says so."

As I prayed, I saw its face change. It pursed its mouth, then its features relaxed and its claws loosened as I broke its grip on the area.

I looked closely at the dragon, then took in the entire expanse of the mountain. Its neck was the dip behind the peak, its body the mountain's huge looming bulk. And right at the back of the mountain, at the site of the track we'd driven up, was its tail. In a flash, I saw a vision of the tail tightly holding a clutch of eggs.

Revelation! It was a Mamma dragon, and it was protecting its young so that, in time, it could unleash them onto the surrounding towns – one for each town.

Timothy and I prayed for the smashing of the eggs; that they would not come to fruition, and would therefore not be able to infiltrate the nearby towns, nor take hold of them. We also prayed that the Mamma dragon would lose her grip on the eggs, and that a barrier would be put up between her and them, so that she could no longer protect them.

It was done. We were finished.

We walked down to the water's edge, where I tossed my now useless "staff" into the lake. I no longer needed it. It was only necessary for that battle.

We drove back to the pub for dinner, then we joined in with the community karaoke night. We ministered to the locals, and enjoyed their company. We told them about Jesus and we sang *Amazing Grace* together. As we sang, the hostess asked,

"Can I join in?" Then everyone in the pub joined in, too. The whole town was singing *Amazing Grace* in the pub.

We said goodbye to the locals, and as we were walking to our car, one lady called out, "Do you want to live in Tullah? There are some nice, cheap houses here."

We knew our work was done. We knew we had blessed the people of Tullah, knew we'd set them free of the bondage they'd been under, and protected their town. We knew we had done God's work.

CHAPTER 34

Baby Bree

Our first year of marriage was lovely. We enjoyed each other's company and got used to sleeping in the same bed. Sometimes, we'd have silly fights over the doona, but we'd always sort it out.

We decided to start trying for a family in December 2012. I knew that if I was going to give birth and look after a child, I needed to be healed of my back problems. So I went up the front at church and asked for prayer.

Some people laid hands on me, while the rest of the congregation prayed from their seats. They were such authentic prayers, I felt a hope and positivity for my healing rise up within me.

After the service, I felt the Lord tell me to run laps around the church, and as I obeyed, my back began to align. When I finished running, I could literally feel myself standing straighter and taller.

If I get pain now, it's because I sometimes forget to stretch after working hard. It's just muscle tightness now, whereas it had been my sacrum continuously dislocating. God has put my bones back into alignment. Praise him!

In March 2013, I became pregnant. I was very excited. I told Timothy and he gave me a hug.

We began preparing for life with a little one. I bought some baby clothes and we organised which hospital to go to. My GP helped us choose an obstetrician, and it wasn't long before we were attending regular obstetric visits.

I told my family about the baby pretty early on because I wanted Mum to know. Mum was very excited. She was a great help during the pregnancy, buying me maternity clothes and even attending the birth.

Candace was excited about being an auntie, and she asked me if I was excited too.

"Yes. I'm a bit nervous though."

In unison, Mum, Grandma and Candace asked, "What are you nervous about?"

"I'm nervous about being a good mummy."

They all chorused, "You'll be great!"

It was so good to hear that they all had confidence in me.

I remember my first scan at six weeks. The radiographer confirmed there was a strong heartbeat.

I kept healthy and fit throughout the pregnancy, taking daily exercise and eating well. By six months, my stomach was really showing. Bree was getting bigger, growing healthy inside me. At seven months I had to stop work. It was just getting too much for me.

During the third trimester, my tiredness increased, because Bree was getting heavy. (Being heavily pregnant is like carrying shopping you can't put down.)

The contractions started in earnest during the night. I really thought Bree was going to come out, so we went to the hospital. I remember standing in the late-night emergency entrance, holding my cramping belly and yelling, "I need to get up to maternity please!"

Once In the ward, the nurse checked my cervix. I wasn't dilated yet, so we went back home.

I was still getting pretty intense contractions at bedtime, so I went to bed with a hot water bottle. Surprisingly, I had a good sleep.

Next morning, I woke up feeling crampy. After breakfast and a walk, the cramps intensified, so I said to Timothy, "I think I'm in labour."

Through the day, the labour intensified. As the pain increased, I dealt with it by singing and dancing. And eventually, by screaming, until the midwife told me to take the energy from screaming and put it into pushing. Finally, Bree came out. The obstetrician cut the cord and laid him in my arms.

In that moment, my pain, (which was still present as the afterbirth slipped out), was temporarily forgotten. I was overcome with joy and love for this tiny human I'd helped create. This little person I was properly meeting for the first time was worth all the pain and effort. It's true what the Bible says, *"A baby is bought into the world through the pain of the mother. But when she holds her child in her arms, her pain is overtaken by the joy of bringing life into the world."*

I started talking to Bree immediately. "Hello Bree! Mummy is very proud of you. You did such a good job coming out my darling. Good work for making it through that tiny tunnel. Mummy's going to take you home and look after you. Daddy will too. Then Mummy's going to teach you how to eat and drink and play, and when you get bigger, Mummy will teach you how to swim. Then you'll get to go to school. Doesn't that sound exciting?"

Dad came to collect Mum. He arrived just as the obstetrician was finishing off my stitches. Normally, I'm quite modest around men. But at this point I didn't care. Four people had just seen me naked, sweaty, singing at the top of my lungs and dealing with labour pains the best way I knew how. They saw me lose control of my bowels with the effort of birth, and they saw a tiny human come out of me. Modesty had long gone out the window!

Even though it was painful, it was truly one of the best experiences of my life.

I was able to enjoy it because I had knowledge of what my body was doing, and because nobody pushed me into doing anything I didn't want to, which allowed me to feel in control of the situation. I had two of the most important people in my life there to support me, and I was able to use natural pain relief. If you've got these things in place, labour can be fun.

I also know that many prayers for a safe delivery were answered that day. I later learned that a family friend had been praying for comfort for Bree and me during the labour, and as she prayed, she felt like she was massaging both our backs. That "prayer massage" definitely worked, because by all medical accounts, back-to-back labour should have been way more painful than it was.

It was a miraculous birth.

Thank you, Lord.

CHAPTER 35

Feeding Pressures

Timothy and I asked the nurses to look after the newborn Bree so we could go for a walk. We were supposed to be having a nice time, but unfortunately, my pelvic floor muscles had taken a beating during the birth. I kept coughing, and my coughing kept causing me to wet myself.

I was really embarrassed and I didn't want Timothy to see, so I walked back to the hospital without him, crying and feeling ashamed. I felt like less of a desirable woman. On top of that, my nipples hurt, my bottom hurt and my private parts hurt.

I just wasn't coping.

The nurses saw me crying and comforted me. Timothy came back soon after, and I apologised for walking away. I told him I was embarrassed about wetting myself, and instead of the judgement on my womanhood I'd been expecting, all he gave me was compassion. He didn't think of me as any less than before. He just wanted to help me. What a relief.

Three days later, just before leaving hospital, I was feeding Bree when I had an epiphany. I was listening to a Christmas album when the song "Sweet Little Jesus Boy" came on. As I realised Jesus had *really* been a tiny, helpless newborn, I suddenly started crying tears of joy. Then I realised that before that, he'd also been a foetus and an embryo. He made himself so vulnerable for us. It's astounding.

Trouble Breastfeeding

Unfortunately, we had great trouble breastfeeding from the very start.

26th September 2013

I asked a second nurse for feeding advice, and now I'm really confused. The nurse yesterday said I should rest and express, which I thought was a good idea. But this nurse told me not to, saying, "You won't do that will you?" Like expressing was a sin.

I don't know what to do. Should I keep feeding him or not?

27th September

We went to the lactation consultant and she said to just switch to formula if feeding wasn't working. She said it's more important that we are all healthy and that we do what's best for all of us. Really helpful.

29th September

This time, the lactation consultant was a different woman. She reckons I need to keep trying to breastfeed. She said I could buy nipple guards from the chemist.

At Mum's place, I was feeding Bree through the nipple guards, and he sucked so hard he made me bleed. I don't want to feed him blood. Mum reckons I should switch to formula. I think I'll give it a couple more weeks and then change if I still can't get it to work. But we'll have to use formula as a back-up for a couple of days until my nipples heal.

31st September
    The lactation consultant reckons I can still feed him breast milk if I'm bleeding. I don't like the sound of that, but I guess she knows best, seeing as this is her job. I'll feed him from the nipple that's not as bad.
    I'm still not feeling that good about it though.

3rd October
    I told the consultant that Bree is not putting on enough weight because he can't seem to latch on properly and that I want to switch to formula. She said I should hire an expressing machine from the chemist, that using it should increase my supply.
    I do not have a good feeling about borrowing this machine at all. Something about it is really unsettling my spirit. I told Timothy this and he reckons I should still give it a go. Ok, I will, but if I don't like it, I'm taking it back.

6th October
    I hate this machine! It hurts! My nipples are bleeding more now. It also makes me feel like I'm basically just a cow; used for my milk supply.
    I swear there's something spiritually wrong with it because whenever I get it out, I feel this wave of depression and trepidation wash over me.

We keep not making it to church because I feel this compulsion to have to use it before we go. We've missed church three times now.

This morning, after I used the machine, I was so stressed, and feeling so much like I was only worth the milk I could produce through it, that I tore my own hair out, literally.

I am taking this thing back and getting a gentle one, new from the baby shop. Who knows what kind of weird spirituality could have been put into it from other women who used it?

I went to the Summer Festival for a while to calm myself down, and it did help, but then, at the supermarket, I fell asleep while pushing a trolley and nearly knocked over a shelf. I sent a desperate prayer to heaven, asking that I get to the checkout without further mishap, and I did make it to a checkout.

The girl was so kind. She let me have a nap on the bench while she sorted the groceries out for me. She even took my trolley up to my car for me. She was an answer to prayer.

7th October

Mum brought me a hand-held expressing machine, and it's so much gentler. It doesn't hurt me. It just gets the milk out. Much more milk too, praise God!

9th October

I told the lactation consultant about my new machine, and that I intend to wean Bree off my milk and onto formula, and instead of being happy for me, she bullied me into trying to breastfeed again. I didn't even realise until I got home and was feeding Bree with a nipple guard on, instead of sticking to my plan. Right, that's it. I'm going off breast milk all together now. I'm not letting her bully me.

10th October

I told Timothy that I was going to switch Bree exclusively to formula and he said he wants me to try to keep breastfeeding. I said I can't and he said to just try for another day.

Ok, I guess I should submit to him. But I don't like this.

11th October

At church I told some other women about my predicament and they all told me to keep on with breastfeeding. I don't think they realise how painful it is for me, or how Bree isn't getting enough to eat because he can't latch on properly. What is it with everyone and breastfeeding? Why can't they accept my decision? Why are they pressuring me? Even Timothy is, and that's the worst part. I thought he was supposed to back me. God, what do I do?

Someone told me to try for one more week, then quit if it doesn't work, so I agreed. I don't know why.

13th October

I was feeding Bree and it was so painful, both physically and emotionally, that I screamed. That made Bree startle and cry. How is this healthy for us?

14th October

Little one is losing weight. The child health nurse said he's losing it far too fast.

15th October

I tried feeding him one more time, but the pain was so bad, it was sending shooting pains into my head. This is not normal.

Timothy came out and saw me really struggling and Bree not able to suck the milk out and he burst into tears.

He kneeled before me and stroked Bree's head and said he was sorry for pressuring me. He said other people had been pressuring him and telling him to pressure me, and he hadn't known what to do, because they were church people and he thought he should obey them. But when he finally realised how bad this was for us, he felt awful that he'd listened to them.

He said he was sorry over and over again, to me and to Bree, and he said, "Please stop breastfeeding. It's not doing you any good. I'll go buy some more formula right now."

We have to stand strong as a family and do what's best for us, not blindly obey others.

18th October

I am now on my way to weaning bubba off my milk. I express three times a day and give him that, but I mainly give him formula.

I do this so that my breasts don't get infected from a build-up of unused milk.

It's hard work, and I'm still not getting enough sleep, but at least it's a step in the right direction.

21st October

I feel sick. I'm all cold and hot and I've noticed a burning sensation in my right breast. I wonder what's going on.

23rd October

I went to the doctor and she said I have a fungal infection. I have to put some weird cream on my nipples and not express for a few days.

24th October
    The hot and cold feeling hasn't gone away, in fact, it's worse now. And the cream doesn't seem to be doing anything. I think I need a second opinion.

27th October
    I have noticed a lump in my breast. I hope it's not cancer. It's hot to touch and sore.

28th October
    GP says I have really bad mastitis, (infection from clogged milk ducts), and that it looks like I've had it for about a week. She said I was misdiagnosed by that last doctor, and if they had treated me for mastitis back then, it wouldn't have got so bad.
    She's given me some antibiotics. I have to take them for a few days, and if there's still no change, I might need surgery to get rid of this lump.

31st October
    Well I have taken all my antibiotics and the lump's huge now, and shiny. The GP sent a letter to the sonographer to fast-track me for an ultrasound. Have to go in tomorrow.

1st November
    I had my ultrasound. It's an abscess. On my breast. It has to be surgically removed. Far out Brussel sprout times infinity! Why do I have to go through this?

2ⁿᵈ November

I'm in hospital, recovering after breast surgery. When I first got here, I was given a bed straight away. The nurse who looked at my lump said, "You're a tough lady!"

I am! And I was a tough lady in danger.

The doctor told me I'd been fast-tracked because I had septicaemia. The infection had spread into my blood. He said he was going to do the surgery at seven p.m., moving it forward by a day, because if he didn't do it fast, I'd die.

Oh my God! I nearly died! From a completely preventable problem. Far out!

3ʳᵈ November

Woke up at nine a.m. and I already feel much better. The surgery has done wonders.

I carefully walked over to the naturopath to buy some sage tea to help me dry up my milk. The less I have to express with a drain in my breast, the better.

When I asked the lady for sage tea, she asked me why I wanted it, and when I told her, she had a go at me, tried to convince me that I should keep breastfeeding, warning me about "the dangers of the sugars" in formula.

I told her that I just had surgery from life-threatening mastitis and she still tried to talk me into feeding.

What is wrong with these people? Why would you pressure me to keep breastfeeding when it was continuing to breastfeed that caused the life-threatening infection in the first place?

Why are they making it the 11ᵗʰ commandment that I breastfeed? Why do they judge me as a bad mother for stopping? It makes no sense. If I died from continuing, how would I be a good mother?

4th November

I'm home, and I'm getting better. I hate this drain in my breast. It's meant to drain out any excess pus. But it hurts, especially when I express.

I'm not supposed to have a shower until it's taken out, but I'm not obeying that. I stink from the infection.

7th November

Some idiots at church are still trying to get me to go back to breastfeeding. After that! What the hell is wrong with you?

I told them that I couldn't feed him breast milk because my milk is now coming out green, (true), and they just acted like I was bad for not breastfeeding. Where's your compassion?

How can you think that my life, even little one's life, is less important than breastfeeding? Which part of "life-threatening mastitis resulting in septicaemia" did you not get? And which part of "Bree's not putting on weight and could also die if she gives in to our demands" did you also not get?

Some people are just so religiously and dogmatically stubborn, with no flexibility or understanding.

25th November

The drain has been taken out and the infection is finally completely gone. And I've weaned little one off breast milk. He's completely on formula now. He's taken to it so well and he's been putting on weight well. Such a relief!

As you can see from this ordeal, I finally overcame the pressure to perform to false standards, and we finally did what was right for us.

You can too. Don't question yourself like I did. You know in your heart what's best, so follow through with that.

Another take away from this story is that God is always there, even when life throws you a massive curve ball. Jesus is always rooting for you, even when the world is being mean to you, even when the church, his people, who are supposed to be the kindest, are acting like the worst bullies.

Thank you, Lord for your providence even through trials and tribulations.

CHAPTER 36

A Row of Miscarriages

May 2017

I'm pregnant again. Yay! I'm so happy to be able to give Bree a sibling. God has blessed us.

Early June 2017

Everything is going OK. No morning sickness this time. Heartbeat strong on scan.

June 14th

I started bleeding. Not heavily. Just light. Should I be worried? I don't think I need to yet. I had spotting with Bree. It'll probably be OK.

June 16th

I'm still bleeding. It's getting heavier. I've prayed that God will help everything be OK. Maybe I shouldn't worry just yet. I should trust God.

June 17th

The blood got heavier this morning, and I started cramping. Now I am worried. Something's wrong. I need to see a doctor.

June 18th

The bleeding is heavy enough to need a pad and I'm in pain. I'm going to hospital. Oh God, I hope I'm not losing the baby!

June 19th

The doctors said that there's a chance I could still keep the baby. They couldn't see any sign of me having already miscarried. They can still hear the heartbeat. I'll pray. Oh Lord, I'm so nervous.

June 21st

I went to my GP. She said my hormones are going down. I'm losing the baby. I am heartbroken. I cried in the doctor's room. This is awful. At least she was kind.

Timothy went quiet. Bree asked what was happening and we had to explain to him that his brother or sister had died. That was the worst part, feeling like I'd let him down.

June 22nd

We rang Nicholas Perry to tell him what happened, and asked if the church could provide some food for us because I couldn't face cooking. When Greg brought some meals for us, Timothy burst into tears, and Greg gave him a hug.

June 24th

We'd already organised to go to family camp. We decided to still go, because it means we'll be surrounded by people who love us, and all our meals will be prepared for us, so I won't have to do much housework or cooking.

June 27th

It was hard being at camp while I was losing a baby, yet having that support around me really helped.

I was soothed by kayaking around the little islands and seeing the natural beauty.

We had intended to camp in a tent, but the leaders gave us a cabin, so I could sleep in a bed. Bree had a good play with some of the other children.

On our second day there, I was in the shower when the baby came out along with a whole lot of blood. The cramps were really painful. I sobbed and sobbed.

I'm so glad I was with friends. I'm not sure I would have got through this without Timothy, Mum, Breanna and my church family.

August 8th

A man at church, who knows we just miscarried, said to me, "When are you going to have more children? You need to have more children." As though there was something wrong with me for not having more yet, as though I was bad for not being able to hold onto the baby, and as though it was my fault. Why would you say that to a woman who is still numb from miscarrying? Such an awful, insensitive thing to say. And why does he think I need more children? I want them, but I can live without more. It's not like my life depends on it. Is he saying I'm not worthy to be called a woman because I lost a baby? That's what it sounded like.

September 12th

I said to a man at church that how many children we have is in God's hands. He looked at me and said, "Isn't there something you can do about it?" Implying that we hadn't been doing that thing, and that me losing our child was somehow my fault for not having enough sex.

Then he said something that implied it was also Timothy's fault for not being "man enough" to demand more sex from me.

Our sex life is not your business, and even if we shagged like rabbits, it's still no guarantee that I'd get pregnant, or bring the baby to term.

Men like this are so frustrating. First, they demand we look and act in certain ways so that we don't turn men on, then they demand we hurry up and get married, then, when we do marry, they try to police how often we "give our husbands" sex! Then they say stupid things like, "When are you going to have children?"

Then it's, "When are you going to have more children?" and then it's, "There's something defective about you, and also something shameful and disobedient, because you didn't keep the babies for your husband, and now we judge you as not wholly woman."

They never actually outright say the last bit, but it's certainly implied.

When I am ever enough for you? Why can't you love me as I am? Can't you see I did everything I could to keep the baby? Just leave your judgement at the door please sir, it's not welcome here!

Thankfully, not many men do this. Only a few. Everyone else was really helpful and supportive.

But it still hurts.

April 4th 2018
I'm pregnant again, at last. After two years. Woohoo! Finally, a sibling for Bree. I was too excited to keep it to myself, so I told the neighbours.

April 10th
Everything is going fine. Some morning sickness, but not bad. Hope it all works out OK.

April 25th
I'm six weeks now. I suddenly got really sick. Can't keep anything down. This sucks.

April 28th
Started bleeding. I collapsed on the stairs, calling out, "No, I can't do this again!" Timothy came running, asked me if I thought I was losing the baby. I said I hoped not.
Went to the GP to get some tests. My hormones were going down, but not by enough for her to be worried. Rallied the troops, asked them to join us in prayer that the baby would survive. I hope to God it works. I can't lose another one.

April 30th
Had a scan and they couldn't see a baby. I started worrying that I had already lost it, but we kept praying anyway.
Called a friend to tell her about the scan, and she said not to let anyone pressure me to have an operation to get rid of the baby.

May 1st

I have asked God to make it clear whether or not the baby will live.

May 6th

In hospital again. The bleeding's very heavy now. It's clear I'm miscarrying. I'm devastated. But still, I'm glad my prayer for clarity was answered.

I asked for another scan, to ensure the baby was dead. There was no way I was having the baby cleared out of me if there was any chance she could live.

They showed me the image. A baby but no heartbeat. It was clear she'd died, so I agreed to the operation. It was successful. Dead baby gone. I was allowed home a few hours later.

May 20th

We are still devastated. It's hard to talk about.

August 5th 2019

I'm pregnant again! I have a good feeling about this one, like this time it will work. I told my neighbours again. Too excited not to.

August 13th

All is going well. No sickness, strong heartbeat, all good. Yes!

September 5th

I'm sick again. Really sick. It's even worse than last time.

September 8th

I had to go to hospital because I'm super dehydrated. I feel like I have the worst hangover in human history. They gave me some meds to stop me vomiting. They haven't kicked in yet. Hope they do soon. They also put me on a drip to rehydrate me. Might be here a while.

September 11th

I'm bleeding again. I'm going to lose her, I can feel it. Oh God, I feel sick! I can't do this! Help!

September 12th

Rallied the troops once again. Please God, hear my prayer! Do something!

September 13th

The bleeding got heavier this morning, now I'm cramping. Bummer.

I suspected I was going to miscarry, so I asked a friend if she could have Bree tonight, in case we have to go to hospital. Then Timothy and I prayed that God would give us a clear sign as to whether the baby would survive or not.

September 14th

I woke up at three a.m. with this weird feeling that there was something in my pants. Went downstairs to the loo, pulled my jammies down and, "plop" went my placenta, onto the floor.

My first reaction was, "Gosh, it's amazing that didn't hurt coming out. It's huge! Thank you God."

I cleaned myself up as best I could. I was feeling pretty calm, until I stood up, then it hit me. I suddenly felt really dizzy, then the horror of what just happened sunk in and I screamed out for Timothy.

He came running and I told him what happened. I began panicking, flailing my arms around and screaming. Timothy ran the shower and helped me into it. I stood under the water, crying, shaking, praying, and letting the water and my Heavenly Father soothe me. Then Timothy helped me out of the shower, into my clothes, and onto the couch with a heat pack and a cup of tea. He picked up the placenta and wrapped it in rags, then buried it.

I got up and went for a walk outside, because even just being in the same vicinity as my lost placenta was too much for me in that moment. While I walked, Timothy packed for hospital. Then he drove me in.

As soon as I got in the car, Timothy prayed that the pain would leave, so that I could cope with the journey, and almost immediately, the pain was gone. We saw some wildlife while we were driving, and we played some games on the hour-and-a-half drive. I started feeling happy and calm again. And the pain did not return until we had nearly reached the hospital. Now that's an answer to prayer.

As soon as we arrived, the intense pain returned. We didn't have to wait long for an emergency bed, and almost immediately, the nurses gave me some pain meds and organised for me to have another D and C.

While waiting for the surgery, Timothy went out for a walk, and I did a drawing to remember Claudia by. We'd named her, because we knew she was a girl. I drew a love heart surrounded by purple patterns, and wrote, "Goodbye Claudia. Have fun in heaven. We will always love you." As I finished the design off, I started sobbing. The nurse came in and comforted me. She *talked to me for a while, then fetched me some blankets and a cup of tea.*

It was even more heart breaking this time, because Claudia had been 13 weeks. I thought she was going to make it. We really thought it was going to work this time.

I felt angry too, because I had been so sick for nothing. It felt like the enemy was having a real go at me.

Finally, the obstetrician came to talk to us about the procedure. Once again, we asked for another scan, to make sure the baby was dead. And once again, there was a baby but no heartbeat.

She was gone.

September 28th

I'm still cramping. This isn't right. I'm going back to see the obstetrician today, and he'll do a scan to see what's happening.

At the scan:

I have a uterine infection, because a tiny bit of the baby was left after the D and C. I have to take antibiotics and have a few days off work. Far out, haven't I been through enough already?

September 30th

Went on Facebook, which was probably stupid, seeing as I'm so emotional right now. This post from Garry hits me, "I can't think of anything more dehumanising than making a woman have a baby when she doesn't want it."

Because I have known Garry for so long, I thought it would be OK to comment. So I posted, "And I can't think of anything more dehumanising than killing a child just because you don't want it!"

I get back, "A foetus is not a child Jules," in this really condescending tone that you could hear even through Facebook.

Science tells us that a baby is a living baby from conception. And I know that abortions may be necessary in emergencies and hard cases, such as rape. I am still friends with my friends who have had abortions. I tried to explain all that, and I even cited some research.

In return, without citing any research, without giving any proof, and without any clarification of his views, Garry told me not to put my religion into the argument, and said nobody should believe an unborn baby is a person, that those who do are hurting others.

I have just miscarried. I know that my unborn baby was a baby. He made it seem like I was bad for grieving the loss of my child, and like my grief didn't matter.

I've blocked and unfriended him.

March 14th 2020

Pregnant again! Told Mum and asked her to pray.

March 20th

I'm really sick again. I had to go to hospital for meds again, and one night, I had to call the ambulance to come and give me an IV drip because I was so dehydrated. Hyperemesis is not nice!

April 20th

8 weeks today.

April 22nd

I started bleeding and cramping again. I had to go to hospital. Because of Covid, Timothy couldn't come with me. I had to go through all the tests and scans by myself. Awful!

The gynaecology team did some tests, poked things up me, which wasn't pleasant. Then they took my blood, and said my hormones were dropping. They gave me some more tests and some pain meds and admitted me to surgery. While I was waiting to be transferred to the operating table, I cried because this was the fifth lost baby.

One of the doctors asked, "What's wrong?"

I replied, "What do you think? I'm losing another baby." Such a stupid question.

Before the D and C, they said they'd send any leftover products to a lab, to see why I keep miscarrying. They also said if there were any remains left after the tests, they'd send them to us so we could bury them and have a funeral. They said we'd get the results in four weeks. Finally, we'll get some answers. Finally, we'll get some closure.

June 1st

I hadn't heard from the hospital about the tests, so I rang them. A young man answered the phone and said that everything was fine.

I said, "No it's not, because I was supposed to hear back about the tests to see why I keep miscarrying. It's been six weeks and I still haven't had a call from you."

I was transferred to Sadie, one of the head midwives.

She said, "I'm sorry to tell you this, but one of the staff has made a big mistake."

She went on to explain that this staff member had been meant to put any remains into saline, but they'd accidentally put them in acid instead. My baby had been burned up. There was nothing left of her. Now I can't even have a funeral for her. And as for finding out why my body keeps miscarrying, Sadie said there are other tests they can do, but unfortunately they aren't as accurate.

I feel so ripped off. And so traumatised.

Sadie said she was very sorry, and I knew she meant it, but that didn't make things any better.

I feel like I've lost my baby twice.

September 9th

It was my last chance to go in for those tests today, but I just couldn't face it. It's too traumatising to go back there; knowing that's where my baby's remains were forever lost.

I don't think I can do those tests.

Maybe I can try again to get the tests in a year or two, then try for another baby. But for now, I just can't. I told Timothy I needed to start using contraception again, and he agreed.

January 12th 2021

I wrote a complaint letter a while back, and today I got a reply. And it's good. The hospital has changed their policies, so that acid is no longer allowed in theatre during D and Cs, and they have clearly labelled the saline, so that staff will have no doubt about what they are putting baby remains into.

They have trained up all their midwifery and gynaecology staff in regard to these changes, ensuring that all staff know the difference between saline and acid, and that they are to send any remains to the lab straight away. Praise the Lord!

They are also going to provide me with free counselling. The woman who wrote the letter was very apologetic, and I could tell she was sincere. I am very thankful for that.

February 4th 2023
My periods have been getting heavier and more painful lately. I started to wonder if maybe I was having another mis- carriage, except I didn't think I was pregnant. Then, today at work, I collapsed from severe period pain, and I mean severe! So my boss sent me home early.
I went to the supermarket to get a few groceries before coming home, and I collapsed again in the store. I had to pray that God would keep me conscious, and help me drive home.
Now I'm in bed with a heat pack, and I've made an appoint- ment to see the GP.

February 6th
I went to hospital with extreme pain. They gave me a CT scan and an ultrasound. I have a fibroid. No wonder I have so much pain. So that's what's wrong.
I still think I have endometriosis too.
They said they can't take the fibroid out now, because the right surgeon isn't available. The young male doctor tried to send me back to the GP for a referral, but I said, "No, I've prob- ably had this problem for ages, and you didn't do anything. Remember last time I came in with the same sort of pain, and I didn't even get any tests done, and you told me I was just overreacting, and to stop making such a fuss? Yeah, well, this is almost as bad as labour pain, so something is clearly wrong."

After that, he looked up the best gynaecologist in Hobart, and he's sent a referral for me.

Sometimes we just have to be firm with these men who think they know everything. They might have gone to medical school, but they don't have female bodies, and I am the expert on my own body. I know something is seriously wrong and needs checking.

I am getting stronger. Go me!

February 13th
I had a follow up scan, and the man who did my scan wrote on my form, "Small fibroid, probably not causing pain." You idiot! How would you know? Is it in your body? I know it's causing pain because I collapsed, twice. Why do these men keep acting like I'm being a hysterical female?

February 19th
I've seen the gynaecologist. He believed me. He explained that fibroids that small don't normally cause pain, so that's why the sonographer may have written that comment, but he didn't disregard my pain, or minimise it.

He asked why I thought I also have endometriosis, but he did it in a curious manner, not a patronising one. I felt heard.

He has booked me in for surgery to get rid of the fibroid, and he said he will also check if there's any endo matter inside me at the same time.

March 6th
I had my surgery. The doctor said he found lots of endometriosis matter, the majority of it in my bowels. He scraped all of it away. So I'll be good for a long while now.

Thank you, Lord!

They found the problem. They found why I kept miscarrying.

I still feel sad that I lost so many babies, and mad that I had to press to be listened to. But I am also glad that someone finally did listen, and that they found the problem.

March 12th

I have finally made peace with the fact that I may never bear another child. I decided to just be happy with Bree, and thank the Lord for him; to focus on Bree's life and the joy he brings me, rather than focusing on our losses.

I still want more kids, but if I don't get to have them, I'm OK.

God brought me to this place, and it's nice to finally be here. Thank you, Lord!

CHAPTER 37

Business and Ministry

Business Blessings

Back in 2005, one of Mum's friends came to stay with us, and one morning, she came into my room, sat on my bed and prophesied that I would run a business. I knew I wanted to sell my art, bless people with it, and use it as a ministry tool. But Gwen also talked about me running creative women's retreats, so I could help women know themselves and God better, and help them unlock their creativity.

I thought it was a brilliant idea, and definitely a God idea, so I started planning.

Within a few months, I'd received the very first orders for my art. A few years later, I ran my first women's retreat at View Town. My goal was to help women know God and themselves more, and to encourage them in their creativity. I believe I achieved this, so I ran three more retreats.

In 2008, I got an increase in orders for my art, beginning with an order for a painting from a regular at Fabulous Café.

In 2012 I began selling at markets. I remember at one market, a lady was admiring my work, when she said something about not feeling confident in her own creativity. I encouraged her, telling her she can make art and that she should keep trying, and I gave her tips on how and where to try selling her work.

While I was talking to her, God spoke to me. He said, "You are a conductor of productivity." He showed me I wasn't just there to make money; I was also there to connect people with their own productivity, and to help them know they can be creative.

In August that year, I entered one of my large silk paintings in the Hobart Show. I won an award for it and a photo of it was put in the paper. God was building momentum.

Next, I started a mailing list for my products, and begun receiving orders from it. And soon after that, I began stocking art print merchandise. I entered lots of community art exhibitions. It increased my exposure, my sales and my productivity.

In 2013, I saw an ad in the local paper asking for stall holders for an art show. This proved hugely successful. I also sought the Lord about finding galleries in which to display my art. I felt God tell me to call a specific gallery in country Tasmania, so I called them. That weekend, Timothy and I went to see him, and he agreed to take my work. It turns out the owners were Christians, and they gave a tithe of their sales to Empart; the same missions organisation we sponsor. How awesome!

In 2015, the Lord led me to buy the newspaper, something I don't normally do. But I knew there was something in it God wanted me to see. I found an advertisement for a new market, looking for stall holders. I realised this was why God wanted me to buy the paper, so I applied and was given a space. It was a great little market.

Later in 2015, I was chosen to be part of a big arts show-case in Hobart. I set up my display with handmade scarves, art print merchandise, drawings and wall art pieces. It was a great night. At one point, I was asked to come up on the stage to talk about my work. I showed my hand drawn colouring books. As soon as I went back to my stall, I sold three books.

I held my first solo exhibition in 2014 at a gallery in Riverton. I showcased silk paintings and scarves of my favourite place, and sold five scarves. My second solo exhibition was at Rhonda's gallery in Plateau Creek. I showcased handmade outfits in the theme of Australian habitats. Then, in December 2015, I held another solo exhibition at the local library and in 2016 at a gallery in Salamanca.

In 2017, I was accepted into two more galleries. Then I was asked to make some work for a tourist attraction. In 2019, I had another exhibition at Rhonda's, for which I made scarves and sarongs. I ran an art workshop as part of it, and taught silk scarf making. I also began at Rocky River markets that year, and it proved very successful.

It's been a great few years of blessing after blessing for my business.

Ministry in Paradise

Bree and I took a well-earned holiday, staying with friends. On the very first night of the holiday, at about three a.m., we were awoken by a huge crash. I thought it was just a car backfiring, but Bree insisted that I go check. I went outside and got a big shock. Our car, which I'd parked on the street, had been hit by another car with such force, it was pushed 10 metres up the road, where it promptly hit a power pole and knocked out the power.

We hired another car and completed our holiday. I wasn't going to let this accident stop us from enjoying ourselves. While we were away, the insurance claim went through. We only received about half what we needed for a new car, so we prayed the rest in. Only a couple of weeks later, we received a letter from Centrelink, telling us they owed us $9,000 because we'd overestimated our earnings. I have never before heard of Centrelink openly admitting that they owe someone that much money, have you? And it happened at just the right time, showing God's hand.

With the combined funds from the insurance money, some savings, more art sales and this miraculous answer to prayer, we bought another car outright. Praise God!

In October 2017, we had to move out of the house we'd been renting for seven years. We really didn't want to move at the time, but now I'm glad we did, because we got to live in the lovely Clear Water River; a remote community on the mouth of the Explorer.

Dad asked God why He sent us so far away and God's answer was that we were sent there as missionaries. This proved to be true.

One evening, Bree was in bed, Timothy was out, and I was settling in for the night when I heard Amanda's ex, Adrian, having a go at her. She was telling him he couldn't come near her, and he was saying, "I'm trying to do the right thing and give you maintenance money for Elizabeth."

Now, to be fair, good on him for actually paying child maintenance. However, Amanda had told him not to come within 10 metres of her home, because he'd previously been abusive. And he had agreed. By coming onto her property, he was disobeying their agreement.

Amanda felt threatened and the argument escalated to a point where Adrian was yelling at Amanda while pushing her, and Amanda was defending herself by telling him off, louder and louder.

I will always stick up for women when men are doing the wrong thing, so I went outside and called out, "Stop speaking to her like that."

Then Adrian began to yell at *me*!

I became very bold.

"No! There is no excuse for speaking to her like that. Get off her property if she doesn't want you there."

He got off her property. Instead, he came onto *our* property and got right in my face, swearing at me and threatening me.

Our neighbours Krissy and Dwight saw what he was doing, and Krissy yelled out, "Adrian, get in your car!"

And after a bit more kerfuffle from him, he drove away.

I met Amanda in the middle of the road to check on her. I asked if she was alright. She was a bit rattled, but she said she was glad of the assistance. I prayed for her, and asked God to enable Adrian to respect her boundaries.

The next day, I called out to Krissy and Dwight to say sorry for any disturbance and they said it was all right.

Another night, I was walking up the road when I felt to stop about halfway and pray that no wolf would be allowed to get through to Amanda's house. I specifically felt to pray for protection for her; that no wolf could come near her or her family or within 10 metres of her property. I marked a line in the dirt, declaring that the wolf could not pass it.

I talked to Dad and Breanna about this later, wondering why I'd felt to pray that specifically. Dad said it might have been Adrian I was praying against. Then Breanna and Dad both said, "Predatory," together.

I was out watering my garden when Selina came into the cul-de-sac, looking for someone who had Panadol and cotton wool, because her brother Keegan had a terrible earache. I gave her some cotton wool and asked her if Keegan would like prayer. I was expecting her to go and ask him, but instead she yelled out, "Keegan, Jules's going to pray for you!" in typical loud Selina fashion.

I went inside and sat next to Keegan, who was lying on the couch. After asking permission, I laid my hand on his ear and prayed that Father God would heal it.

I asked Keegan how it was feeling and he said it was a bit better, so I kept praying.

Then I asked how it felt again. He said it was feeling better, so I checked. The redness in his ear had gone. It looked healthy again.

I said thank you to God and then instructed the family to say thank you too. It was a miracle.

We gave Selina and Roy a car because God told us to bless them. We weren't using that car and they needed it, with six kids. It's amazing how God can use us when we are open to his prompting.

We really feel that we blessed that neighbourhood with our presence, our generosity of spirit and our kindness. We shared our faith. We made an impact on that place.

CHAPTER 38

Memories...

There has been so much trauma in my life, and up until 2020, I did not remember much of it. I put it to the back of my brain, buried it like so many survivors do.

It was only when I started remembering it all in 2020 that I could begin to put the pieces together, and answer some of the traumatised questions from the little girl versions of me.

Re-parenting myself has helped me begin to move beyond the trauma and find myself anew.

Jules' Diary, January 2020 - April 2023

January 20th 2020

I don't know why but I've been thinking about Samson. I was thinking about that counselling appointment I had about him; how I told the counsellor that he put his hands down my undies and started touching me there; how I told her, "He didn't even ask me first."

I had a revelation the other night. I sat bolt upright in bed, said to myself, "That was rape." Then went back to sleep. I'm glad to have finally realised it. But it is still pretty nasty and confronting.

January 24ᵗʰ

Breanna and Andrew got married today! We had a great time! We had wood-fired pizza and donuts and Bree played on the playground. I had a good catch up with some old friends, including Johanna, who asked me, "Do you have a lot of trauma?"

I said yes. It was the first time I'd acknowledged it.

I mean there's the evil spirit raping me, then Uncle Shark, then Samson, then lots of random harassment from men in pubs and boys at school, then Phil, then the row of miscarriages.

That's a lot!

I started shaking a little bit, and I realised I'm more traumatised than I thought. I better get some counselling.

February 19ᵗʰ

I've been having flashbacks; the memories of what Samson did play like a movie in my mind. I can see the scene playing before my eyes, but I can't turn off the TV.

The last one was about him touching my breasts without asking, that time at our house in Gulawayn. And I remembered how confused I was about whether I'd given consent or not, which I reckon he did deliberately to get his way. I had more flashbacks about him throwing me on his bed, taking my clothes off without asking, pinning me down with his legs and touching my breasts without consent.

When I see that image, I cry and I feel sick. Why did I ever think what he did was OK?

February 20th

 I've been to see the doctor. She tested me for anxiety and depression, and I came out with a score of high anxiety. She said it was likely I have PTSD too. She sent a referral to the sexual assault counselling service. Good. I need to see someone.

February 28th

 I am on a waiting list to see SASS. A long one. I understand that there are other assault survivors who may need to be seen before me. But really, three months. That's not good enough for someone so anxious and distraught.

March 1st

 Another flashback. This time about that weird conversation where he said he wanted to rape someone. There's something niggling in the back of my brain about something really gross and creepy he did. I can see him standing at the bottom of the stairs that lead up to the girl's change rooms, but I can't quite put my finger on it.

 Come on brain, help me out! I want to remember!

 I prayed tonight, asking God to allow me to remember whatever he wants and needs me to, so that I can heal. I also asked him to allow me to permanently block whatever he deems too painful for me.

 I trust in God and I know he'll answer my prayer, but I have a feeling I need to see it all, remember it all, in order to heal, and that this is how God is going to pull me through.

March 2nd

Started researching psychopathy and sociopathy. Read up on the symptoms. Samson ticks every box. Uncle Shark seems to tick all the boxes too. We really were in danger.

I'm shaking again.

March 4th

I've been doing some more research. The more I read up on it, the more I am convinced that Samson was/is still a psychopath.

Today I looked at a website about the way psychopaths have romantic relationships. They basically all follow this pattern: idolise, devalue, abuse, discard.

Yep, that's pretty much how Samson treated me.

Remember how he worshipped me at the start, and I had to tell him not to?

Devalue; yep, he did that too.

Abuse; very definitely! That's what all that sexual assault was.

Discard; Yep. He left me for someone else because I wouldn't have sex with him.

March 6th

I've been doing some research on how prevalent sexual abuse and rape is among schoolgirls. How many have been raped?

I watched The Hunting Ground. *Very helpful and a great movie, but gosh it's awful what's happening to these kids. Not just to the girls, the boys too.*

I've been praying against the spirit that is coming against these kids, and praying that it would stop.

March 7th

I've decided to write a teaching series for young people, explaining what assault, rape and harassment are. I can see from my research that a lot of young girls even in Australia experience the kind of things I did. If I can help them by giving them this information, that's good.

Thank you for this gift of writing God. It's really helping me deal with all this. And you are using me to help others. Thank you.

March 9th

I want to vomit. Seriously, I feel physically ill. I've remembered that niggling memory. He followed me up to the girls changerooms! Pretended he just wanted to talk, lied about being there to talk to Nelly.

Somehow, this seems even worse than the rape because it shows how premeditated the rape actually was.

Why did I go out with him? Why did I say yes? Why did I not see the thousands upon thousands of red flags?

Perhaps I should research why young girls can get so tricked. Perhaps it wasn't my fault my brain was so addled.

March 11th

I had to call Lifeline. These memories are so overwhelming, I've been thinking about killing myself.

Thank goodness for Timothy.

March 14th

According to my research, abusers do a thing called love bombing; where they shower you with gifts and compliments to start with, and idolise you. But they also throw a few creepy incidents in early on, so you'll feel confused from the start.

Then, over time, they start dropping the mask, and the abuse gets worse and worse and escalates until they act out whatever their original, evil plan for you was. So it's clear that it wasn't actually my fault at all. He deliberately confused me, gaslighting me.

I was an innocent sixteen-year-old with hardly any experience, who was taught to be nice and give people another chance. I had no idea anyone could be so cruel. No wonder I didn't leave him. I was taught that I had to forgive him.

Ignoring wrongs is not forgiveness at all, but I didn't know that at sixteen. I'm starting to learn that real forgiveness includes acknowledging the hurt done, naming it for what it was, feeling the hurt it caused and choosing to give it to God. It's for my own mental health. It's actually not got that much to do with him.

Real forgiveness does not say "It's OK." Rather, it says, "That was far from OK, but I choose to give it to God and I choose not to hate you anymore, because that's only hurting me. I choose to let God carry it."

It's time for me to let this go. God, I give you this filthy backpack of shame that Samson put on me, because he was too lazy and selfish to take responsibility or carry his own shame. I lay it at your feet because it's far too heavy for me. Please get Samson to carry it himself now.

I should pray for him. It can't have been nice being in his head.

Please heal him God, forgive him Jesus. Please give me your forgiveness for him, because I have none of my own.

Actually, what I want is to smash him in the face! I need to find a way to safely and appropriately express this anger.

March 12th

The flashbacks are getting worse. I can't sleep properly. I'm having nightmares about him. Sometimes they relate to the actual lived experience, other times they are just my brain making up horrible things for him to do to me in my dreams.

I know it's probably some type of processing thing, but I don't like it. I don't want to see his face in my dreams.

March 17th

I am learning about triggers. I did not know this was a thing until recently, when I was told by my counsellor. Apparently, trauma survivors can be triggered by physical things that remind them of the trauma, sounds or gestures, such as face masks, certain songs or movements, and these triggers can send them right back to the traumatic event, so that they relive it.

That's what's been happening to me.

So far, I know my triggers are men with long hair, a certain style of men's clothing, loud banging noises and the song, Play that Funky Music. I haven't been able to listen to that song for years without reacting, because he played it while assaulting me. I used to love dancing to it. Now I can't.

The counsellor gave me some strategies to help me get out of reliving the traumas; like breathing deeply and being present in the moment, getting some exercise or taking a hot bath. She encouraged me to find things that would help me.

I've got my harp, my art, Timothy and Bree. I've got Mum and Breanna, Candace and Dad and my church family. I've got my faith. I've got cups of tea and swimming and walking and hot baths and my Bible.

March 19th

That was the worst trigger ever! I thought I was getting better!

I was at the supermarket when I saw someone who looked like him.

I froze. My breathing became shallow. I nearly ran out of the store. I held my ground and told myself it wasn't him. That was enough to keep me in the store, but not enough to stop me having a complete panic attack. I started shaking and couldn't stop. I was shaking so hard, the trolley I was pushing was rattling. I had to stand still for a few minutes and just breathe, tell myself I was not at his house, I was not sixteen anymore, I was not being raped.

I'm trying to implement what the counsellor told me, but it's really hard to retrain my brain and body out of trauma.

I feel so exhausted after I have a bad flashback or trigger. Especially if I've had the shakes. Then I feel like I've run a marathon or been hit by a bus.

I am not coping with ordinary tasks. I can't seem to get up to get Bree to school, and I can't seem to do housework like I used to.

March 20th

I've been talking to Josie about what happened to me. Funny thing is, since I've started talking to her, other women have disclosed to me the awful things that happened to them at the hands of men. It's like my openness is enabling other people to talk.

On the one hand, I'm really mad at the inherent sexism of our culture that allows so many women to be hurt by men, and so many men to think it's OK to act like women are their property to be used. But on the other hand, I'm glad God is using me and my story, to help others. I think my story is really important, that it might change a few lives, hearts and minds.

March 21st
At today's counselling appointment, the counsellor wouldn't listen. She interrupted whenever I started talking about what happened, and butted in with anti-trigger techniques. I thought the whole point of a counsellor was to listen.

Anti-trigger techniques are great, but I know that what I need is to talk. To tell my story. I've been shut down for so long; I cannot bear to be shut down again.

If I don't talk about it, I swear I'll go mad. Why is this woman, plus the pastor at church, trying to shut me up? Don't they know I have to talk to be healed?

March 30th
I talked to Josie again today, about some new memories, and she again opened up to me about what happened to her. I'm glad God is using me to help other women. He's using me even though I am not fully healed yet.

April 1st
Another flashback, this time while I was cutting the vegetables for dinner. I suddenly saw him sticking his fingers into me, then leaning over me while trying to give me non-consensual oral sex. I remembered how I wanted to scream, cry, run away and tell him he was stupid all at once, but I was completely frozen and couldn't make a sound. It's awful, remembering how disempowered I was. I was trapped there, with him.

I started convulsing. I had to put the knife I was using down. I could no longer cook the tea. I had gone back into shock.

Just as I thought the shock was passing, I remembered that I thought he was going to put his penis in my mouth. I nearly threw up.

April 2nd
I'm still recovering from last night's flashback. I'm still all shaky. My muscles have gone all limp from exertion.

I need this to stop God. Can I have a break from remembering it all please?

April 6th
I remembered that he stalked me in order to ask me out. Following me for that long is not normal, and nor is the way he was so determined to get to me, power-walking to me like he was on a war mission or something.

April 11th
Had another counselling appointment. She listened a bit better this time. But she still interrupts.

May 4th
I've talked to the counsellor about the "golden shower" incident that I'd remembered in another flashback. She agrees it's disgusting. She said he sounds like a psychopath.

May 8th
I told Mum that I realised he was grooming me. She said, "I had that word before you even said it."

Yep, grooming is most definitely the word.

May 10th

I had to call Lifeline again. The realisation that it was actually rape is doing my head in. I need help. I think I need more than the SASS.

May 15th

I pray for Samson a fair bit now, too. I want him to be healed. He was clearly sick. No one can do that sort of thing and be mentally well.

I wonder what drove him to it.

May 18th

Really struggling today, but I am pleased to see that God is still using me to help others. That is the glory of his name. He always wants to help others and he always uses bad for good. That's the God we serve.

I am determined to find something to be thankful for each day, even if it is just that I managed to get out of bed. That's an achievement some days.

May 19th

Poor little Bree is picking up on my trauma and getting scared too, or grumpy. He picks up on emotions so easily, and can sense the atmosphere in a room.

I hope he'll be OK. I've done my best to shield him from this, but I can't stop him from sensing atmospheres. I can't stop him from knowing something is wrong with Mummy or worrying about me. All I can do is comfort him and tell him that Mummy is not OK right now, but she will be. That I have God and Daddy and other people to help me. That Mummy is safe.

I can't do much more. I hope it's enough.

June 4th

I remembered about that party, and how Arabella said, "You've got him wrapped around your little finger."

It made me realise something.

He deliberately played the part of the totally devoted boyfriend who would do anything for me, so that if I told anyone how badly he was treating me, they wouldn't believe me. He was covering his tracks.

Then I remembered the conversation I had with him when he asked me out, how he said, "Ray likes you too, but I told him to let me go out with you, because I like you more."

When I realised the implications of this, it made me shudder. He didn't want Ray to ask me out because he had already planned on raping me. And he didn't want to risk me agreeing to go out with Ray because that would muck up his plans.

June 6th

I've been wondering whether to report him to the police. I think it's important I do. It may help me move on, get some closure.

I'm worried that he may have done this to somebody else; that I may not be his only victim. It makes me feel a real sense of menacing foreboding. I hope he hasn't, but I really think he has. I mean, it's likely, isn't it? Do that as a teenager and you're probably going to get a taste for it, you'll want to do it again.

It makes me shudder, as if a big cockroach just crawled on my face.

CHAPTER 39

Reporting the Crime

June 20th 2020

I have decided to report Samson. I think it's the right thing to do. I can't have the possibility that he's done this to someone else on my conscience. I just can't. I know there's a risk that he'll track me down and hurt me, or at least verbally hassle me if he finds out, but I think it's a risk I have to take. I couldn't bear to hear about another woman being hurt by him, knowing I could have done something to stop him but didn't.

June 21st

I've talked to Mum and Dad and Timothy about reporting him and they all agree it's a good idea, but say that I'm not ready yet, that I need to prepare.

I'm not sure what I need to do to prepare, but I suppose I should at least work on being less emotional when I talk about it. That's going to be hard.

July 5th

I have remembered that voice changer. It makes me angry and disgusted, all at once. Why on earth would you even have one?

I still don't believe it was for music. If that were true, he wouldn't have used it to disguise his voice to tell me he wanted to get me into bed. And he definitely wouldn't have lied to me about doing so.

If he really just had it for music, why would he have needed to pretend he said something else? Why say, "It's good that you didn't hear what I said," when I was trying to get him to be honest with me?

What that shows is a complete lack of honesty and respect.

He was clearly testing me, to see how much he could get past me, to assess how easy I'd be to rape. I feel all agitated in my spirit again; disquieted and disturbed, like I want to throw up, spit out and scream all at once.

July 17th

The counsellor is going to help me prepare for reporting to the police. She says the more factual I can be, the better. I can use what I wrote about what he did as a guide, but just tell the facts, rather than all the emotions. I'll read through my report again, get rid of some of the swear words.

July 30th

One week till the big day. Mum is coming with me. I am really nervous. The counsellor assured me that the police are different these days; that they take these cases seriously now, not just blame the woman. I hope she's right.

Mum read through my diary and even she said it made her sick. She said, "It's horrific."

August 1st
The day is drawing nearer. I'm trying to stay calm, but this is not going to be easy. I have asked a team of trusted Christians to hold me up in prayer. There's no way I can do this without prayer.

August 7th
I did it! I reported him! Well done, Jules!
It went pretty well. The police officers listened and only asked a few questions. I did feel a bit alarmed when one of the questions asked was, "What were you wearing?" But the support lady from SASS didn't seem worried, so I decided not to be either.
I do hope everything is OK. It seemed to go well. Hopefully something can be done about it.

August 8th
The police officer rang me today and told me that every-thing Samson did was my fault because I was wearing a skirt. She reckons I consented because Samson asked, "Do you want to do something else for a while?" That does not mean I consented, that means he asked a question. And he asked it after the fact.
That does not, and never will, equal consent.
She also said it wasn't wrong that he wanted to look at my private parts, because, and I quote, "There's a whole porn industry based on that's what men want to look at." How does

that make it OK? It does not. The whole porn industry is based on sexism and abuse. None of it is OK!

She followed all of that by saying he didn't stalk me. Watching someone for months, following them, perving on them, that's the actual definition of stalking. He definitely stalked me.

I got off the phone and went for a desperate power walk, crying all the way. The counsellor was wrong. The police do still blame women. They don't take it seriously. They think it's OK what happened to me.

I started doubting myself, until a friend, a lovely older woman, reassured me that I was assaulted and raped. She comforted me and prayed for me and told me I'd be OK if I kept working with God towards healing. That's what I'm planning on doing, staying with God all the way.

God showed me a picture recently. In that vision, I had to go back out through a tunnel I'd walked into, because it was blocked at one end by fallen rocks. I had to retrace my steps along the path I was on, back out of the tunnel the way I'd come in. Once back out of the tunnel, Jesus led me alongside the outside wall of the tunnel, to the back of it, then out through the surrounding desert and on between two tall hills, towards a forest. Jesus was leading me all the way. That tunnel was my past and Jesus was guiding me out of it.

I won't be alone in this valley of the shadow. I will be led through it by Jesus, and I need to trust him all the way.

August 12th

I have decided to write a complaint letter about this police officer. She needs to be trained in how to treat survivors, how to speak to them. And she needs to be taught what assault actually is.

I researched what classifies as rape and assault in legal terms.

Rape: any penetration without consent, including with a finger (what happened to me) or an object, and including being forced to penetrate another.

Assault: Forced touching of your private parts by someone else, including breasts, chest, bottom, vagina or penis; or being forced to touch those of another. Also includes non-consensual kissing.

I checked several legal websites and they all said the same thing. I was assaulted three times, and raped once. That's four crimes against me, Samson, and I reckon we're not done counting.

The police were definitely wrong.

I've asked a friend who's a lawyer to read through my account and check whether I'm correct. Can't wait to hear back.

August 24th

Heard back from the lawyer. Yep, I was right. I can use what he says as a basis for my complaint letter, to show that even legal websites and a working lawyer disagree with that policewoman; showing how wrong it was of her to dismiss me. She should have passed my case on to the Director of Public Prosecutions (the DPP).

September 19th

After many drafts, and much editing, the letter of complaint is finally right and sent. Hope it does some good. Hope it helps *more women. Please go before that letter Lord, and allow it to make changes where changes need to be made.*

Timothy prayed over it, and Marigold and Josie prayed too. Hope the prayer covering does something.

I want this letter to make positive changes for women, especially young ones, who don't have the same strength, confidence and ability to call out wrongs as I do. I can make a difference with my writing. Thank you, Lord, for making me who I am.

I was told I wasn't good enough, pretty enough, submissive enough, hairless enough – just not enough, *for so long. But at the same time, I was "too much". Too sexy, too confident, too good, too holy, a goody two shoes, too "frigid" whatever the hell that was supposed to mean. I reckon it means horny, entitled young men can't handle women like me saying no. Learn to deal with your own sense of aggrieved entitlement instead of getting all mopey when beautiful women use their autonomy and "dare" to say no to you.*

And as to "too good", there's no such thing. How can there be too much goodness, a fruit of the Holy Spirit that the world needs much more of? It's ridiculous the "insults" that have been used against me over the years, simply because I said no to something. (I don't count being called "too good" as a real insult, do you?)

September 26th

Heard back from the commissioner. He said it was wrong of that police officer to speak to me like that, that she definitely should not have failed to hand it to the DPP, because it wasn't her decision to make. He also said she should have told me straight up that it needs to be handled interstate, because it happened there. He wants to meet with me to discuss what actions need taking.

Yes!

Someone (in power) is listening to me.

CHAPTER 40

Visions and Healing

I've gone years not only blaming myself, but also blaming God, because I thought he'd abandoned me. I've asked him so many times, "How could you have let that happen?"

Turns out God absolutely did not want any of it to happen, but he gives us all free will and he has to respect and guard that. He can't claim to let us have free will, then come down all guns blazing, demanding complete obedience. That would make him a tyrant. Rather, he works with our free will, respecting this, his gift, in every single person.

Unfortunately, some people chose to do real evil with their free will. Samson was one of those people.

It's not God's fault Samson didn't listen to him. God told me he tried to tell Samson to leave me alone, tried to tell him to forgo his evil plans, but Samson didn't listen. He was determined to do the wrong thing.

So I can forgive God now too, for what I thought he did wrong. I can let that go and place the blame squarely where it's due, on Samson's shoulders.

God gave me a vision to help me understand what was happening. In the vision, Samson was a big, black, hairy spider with bright blue and red marks on his back. I was the most beautiful butterfly Samson had ever seen.

I captivated his attention with my freedom, my love and care for others, my faith in a God he didn't believe in, my colours. He couldn't take his eyes off me, and he decided he had to have me.

But because he was already so perverted and twisted, he could not dream of loving me truly, could not conceive of learning to be free like me, of learning to fly in the grace that is God's love, nor of showing the world God's wonderful, beautiful glory. He could not dare to hope that he too could one day have the colours and the joy of true freedom.

He wanted to fly like me, to fly free with me, but he didn't know how, so he stuck to the world of darkness he knew. Instead of learning to become a butterfly himself, flying free in glory, he let the wicked spider spirit within him take over, and agreed with it to come and get me for lunch.

He started by saying: "I'm not a perv, I'm not a perv, I hope you don't think I'm a perv" injecting his poison. His poison made me numb, so affected by it that my senses became impaired. My spiritual sight was blinkered, my spiritual hearing and discernment were dulled, my spirit voice – the voice of the warrior princess – was partially muzzled, as if a damp cloth sprinkled with chloroform were wedged inside my mouth, stopping my protests and warnings.

When his first trap didn't catch me completely, and he was in danger of seeing me fly away, free again, he tried another tricky trap, and another, and another, until he had me so confused I didn't know which way was up.

The butterfly got caught in the web, because she had lost sight of her compass, and she panicked when she could not find her way out. Her wings were tied. Slowly, she succumbed to the terrible fate of being trapped by those filthy silken strands, so soft, yet so harsh.

She quivered with the effort of trying to get free, but the silky strands were too strong, so she lay still and frozen, waiting for the spider to pounce.

When the spider did pounce, she had a sudden bout of energy and tried to fly free again. She almost got there, but the spider's legs were too strong and hard, and he would not let her up. So she lay there, continuously being hurt by the sick, twisted, evil spider.

At one point, she was free of his claws, so she made one last attempt to escape. But he locked her in with his threats, and she went quiet and still, and succumbed again, just waiting for it to be over.

He set his final, nearly fatal trap: The ill spoken words, "I love you, you're beautiful, thank you for doing this for me," spun the toxic silk around and around the beautiful butterfly's body, heart and mind.

But then an angel came to save her. It stood at the door of the room with a sword in its hand, and looked sternly at Samson the spider. It began to wield the sword through the air, changing the atmosphere with its Godly warlike presence, all the while praying hard for the scared young butterfly.

When, with one phrase, the spider joined in with the demon that had hurt the butterfly years before, the butterfly shook free of the poison of his words. The angel swung his sword and cut away some of the webs around her and with one holy look he made that demon flee!

The spider was slowing now, less powerful without its evil ally.

The angel's voice led in the King! He stood at the foot of the bed, gleaming golden scimitar drawn, holy rage showing clearly on his face for what had and was being done to his holy warrior princess. He walked forward, struck at the spider to get him out of the way, then put his sword down and took out some scissors. With them he gently cut away the webs that had trapped the butterfly.

First he freed her legs, then her private parts, then her feet. Then he cut a line through the mass of silken thread covering her forehead, and with one movement he pulled it all away.

She was free. No longer the spider's prey.

Interestingly, the sticky threads could not adhere to her face, heart, breasts or neck.

Because Jesus lives inside my heart, no evil can stick there! How great is our God!

As the spider's plan was thwarted, and he didn't achieve his end goal (a goal that I believe was my rape followed by my death), he grew tired of it. He discarded his beautiful butterfly and found another spider to mate with. And she was just as perverted as he.

CHAPTER 41

The Warrior Sounds
the Trumpet

October 1ˢᵗ 2020

I am still rejoicing about how God saved me. Definitely worth celebrating! I've decided to play worship songs on my harp more often.

It's nice to have something to be joyful about again.

October 26ᵗʰ

Had the meeting with the commissioner.

He has already reprimanded the police officer who dismissed my case, and he also made her have a talk with her supervisor. She has been warned that if she dismisses assault and rape again, she will be given enforced time off and will be forced to attend police sensitivity training. If she refuses to change her attitudes and behaviours, she will be dismissed.

My letter made positive changes! That's what I was hoping for, that's what I prayed for. Praise God!

The commissioner also told me that my case can be sent to NSW police. I said I'd rather go up and report him to them in person. I don't want news of Officer Sharon not taking me seriously to cause any officers up there to doubt me. Best to start afresh.

November 10th
I have stopped seeing the counsellor I didn't like and started seeing a psychotherapist. She lets me talk and she listens, and she even does some body work with me. I've been reading The Body Keeps the Score, *and I now want to get whatever trauma I'm holding in my body, out.*

November 17th
Second psychotherapy session. Brilliant! She wants us to unpack each incident. I think that's a good idea. So far, a lot of trauma has come out and been processed just about the first few months of knowing him. Thanks for leading me to this woman, God. You sure answered my prayer.

November 24th
We worked through the memory of the, "golden shower," incident. I told her it made me feel cheap, terrified and disgusted. She said to let it out, so I was coughing and coughing, as though I was going to vomit. But it wasn't vomit, it was trauma. I'm glad I got rid of the dark spiritual residue left over from him doing that.
Told her this was one of my worst memories.

December 1ˢᵗ

My therapist says I am doing really well, that I'm working hard at my healing, which enables her to release things from me.

A professional said that I'm doing well! I'd better start believing it! Timothy always tells me, but I doubt him. I shouldn't.

I should tell myself that more often. I need to believe it.

December 8ᵗʰ

I have a mental health care plan now, which means the government will reimburse me for six sessions. Thanks, Australia!

I've also seen the GP again and she said I definitely have PTSD; she's just not sure which type. I'm not scared of this anymore. It's actually good to get the diagnosis. It explains a lot of things.

Another session done; this time about the actual rape day. Horrible to call it that but there you are, it's true.

The therapist gets me to grab a bat and hit a big mat sometimes. We did that today. I pretended the mat was Samson. Boy, that felt good! Sometimes she gets me to tell him off. I feel like I am getting to say all the things I wanted and needed to say to him back then.

Little by little, session by session, I am getting better, getting closer to full healing.

December 15ᵗʰ

In the session today, we talked about how Samson's brother knew he raped me, yet he still called me a slut.

She put two teddies on the couch next to me; one for Samson, one for Jolly. I told them off and bashed the stuffing out of them.

I think I need to start a kickboxing class or something.

December 20th
Last session for the year. We talked about Uncle Shark and what he did to Candace. I think parts of this trauma are worse than what Samson did to me. We talked about me feeling responsible for Candace's spiritual welfare for years, because Dad let me down that day by not taking charge, and left a 14 year old to deal with it.

She suggested I talk to Dad about how I'm feeling. A good idea.

December 29th
I talked to Dad, told him that I realised I'd been mad at him for years for not taking charge. He said he was sorry for that, that he realises he ought to have.

I feel much better that we sorted that out.

March 13th 2021
I talked to someone from Safe Schools in NSW about what happened to me, and asked if it would be worth sending in a formal complaint. She said yes. I have another letter to write.

I'm taking boxing classes. Me, the only girl in a class of big strong men. Today's class was good, only I couldn't handle the bit where we had to stand still while being punched lightly in the stomach. It's meant to condition us for fights.

It reminds me of Phil, how he used to hit me there.

A friend asked me if I was OK, and I said I was just a bit triggered. I told him I'm a domestic violence survivor who has PTSD.

He gave me a hug. I decided it was best to tell the trainers too.

March 20th
I have written the letter of complaint, and got it edited. I explained that the teachers who saw Samson's inappropriate behaviour should have done more; that he showed no duty of care. I mentioned that it wasn't OK for that student teacher to put all the onus on me to change the situation. Instead, they should have told Samson not to treat me badly, or offered me help to get out of the relationship safely.
I asked for changes to be made to the way sex ed is taught in schools, and for teachers to have to follow duty-of-care procedures properly.
I also asked for the teachers in question to be sought out and made to officially and formally apologise to me.
I think I did a good job with the letter. I hope it's received well, and that something is done about it. I need an apology from the teachers, or at least from the education department, so I can have more closure.

March 27th
Heard back from Steph, the woman from Safe Schools. She is trying to track down the teachers in question.
She assured me that things are different now; that consent is taught comprehensively to all classes, and that the facts about assault and rape are covered. She said that kids are aware these days, and that there are better rules around duty of care. She said that teachers who see or hear dodgy things have to report them now. They can't just let them slide.
This is fantastic news.

April 4th
    Another boxing class. This time I joined in with the entire sparring session. The teachers said I'm doing well. I'm improving and healing. Thank you, God! I knew kickboxing was a good idea.

May 7th
    Today I received a letter from the Department of Education. It was an apology on behalf of the school and the teachers. They acknowledged my pain. They said they're sorry it happened, sorry the school didn't do more at the time.
    Celebration time!

June 7th
    I have decided that I definitely will report Samson to NSW police. I rang the police station closest to where it happened, and spoke to a detective who will take my case.
    I'll ask lots of people to pray.

December 2021; the big report
    We flew up together as a family yesterday, and today I gave my statement to the detective. My mother-in-law came to support me, which was great. I didn't want Timothy to have to hear it all again, or see me in such distress.
    Terry, the officer, responded much better than Officer Sharon. He took me seriously, asking lots of questions, and taking down lots of detail. He didn't ask inappropriate questions either. He didn't ask if I'd been drunk, as if that were an excuse, the way she did.
    He did ask what I was wearing that day, but when I asked him why he needed that information, he answered, "I just want

to get as much detail as I can, so that I can ask others who may have been there that day to confirm what you were wearing. It's not to make excuses for him or anything. I know your clothing choice doesn't change his actions."

It was so validating! It clearly showed that he was simply getting detail, rather than using my clothing choices as an excuse.

He was thoughtful and caring. He allowed me to take my time. He didn't rush me. He let me share the details I needed to. Not once did he shut me down.

At about 10 o'clock, he let us take a break and made us some tea. I really needed that.

After I reported the strangling, I felt shaky and distressed, so I asked if we could take a lunch break. I didn't want to break down in front of the police officer. Mum took me to a nearby restaurant for lunch and I burst into tears and nearly threw up. Finally, I could let go of some of the strangulation trauma.

One of the waitresses saw I was distressed, and gave me a note that said, "You are loved."

After lunch, we went back to the police station to finish the report. I told the officer how Samson forced me to have a semi-naked shower with him, how he locked me in the house and held me captive, how he raped me on his sister's bed, and lied to his grandfather.

It wasn't pleasant to talk about, but it was important for me to report. I'm glad I did it.

The detective said he'll talk to Samson and he'll contact the school and the teachers I mentioned. He also said he'll do a welfare check on Samson's wife and children. I'm so pleased about that. Even if the investigation doesn't lead to a court case, at least I know I've told the police what he's like, what *he's capable of, and warned them that he is still potentially dangerous.*

At least they will have checked on his family.

I have stayed true to the watch and given the warning. I have sounded the trumpet, raised the alarm, and lit the beacons. I have done my duty. I have not been idle. And I am proud of that!

CHAPTER 42

Recovery

Jules' Diary 2020 - 2023

February 1st 2020

I made a table that shows the lies I believed about myself for years on one side of the page, and the truth about myself, as God sees me, on the other. When I look at it, I can clearly see the lies for what they are. For example, I was never a bad girl. I am, and always have been, a good girl.

Now I can begin to retrain my brain to believe the truth about myself instead of believing the lies.

February 14th

I've been doing some research on the state of freeze. Apparently there are three stages to it, and by the looks of it, I went through each stage when Samson was hurting me. I was in deep freeze, that's why I didn't fight back or run away. I actually couldn't, because my brain had put all but my basic bodily functions into a state of suspended animation.

I froze to protect myself, because fight and flight hadn't worked. I can stop asking myself why I didn't leave or lash out at Samson. I couldn't, because I was frozen.

February 2ⁿᵈ 2022

I was driving in the car when I had this feeling that there was a spirit inside me, to do with the strangulation. I asked God, "What is it?"

He said it was a spirit of perversion and choking that was still there because of the act of strangulation done against me by Samson.

I prayed for this thing to be gone in Jesus' name. Then I started coughing and felt it come out of me. I saw it sitting on the floor, in the passenger seat foot well. It was looking at me. It was black and featureless, like the creature from the black lagoon. It had a chain around its neck and that chain was attached to me; the chains other end tied around my neck!

It started pulling on the chain, trying to get me to choke, so I told it to stop in the name of Jesus, told it to let go. I was searching for something to cut the chain with and Jesus said, "Just use your sword," so I picked up my sword of the spirit and cut the chain free. Now the demon was no longer chained to me.

I pulled the remaining chain still around my neck off, and told the demon to get out of the car and go back to hell where it belongs. It got right down, flush with the floor, turned itself into a puddle of ooze, and slid under the door and out of the car to get away from me.

I am free from a demon of choking. Thank you, Lord!

February 8th

Only a week since I got rid of that demon of choking and already I can feel a big difference. When I got home that night, after praying, I could do the dishes. I could do housework! I haven't been able to for months, I just haven't had the energy. But now I can.

April 16th

At kickboxing tonight, we did some wrestling practice. I was thrown to the floor by one of the guys, and I didn't even cry. That's how far I've come!

March 23rd

Wrestling again at kickboxing tonight, and this time, I threw Larry to the ground! Wow! I didn't know I was so strong. And I didn't know I got that brave. I am really proud of myself!

April 2nd

I had a phone call from the detective. He's spoken to Samson, who has denied it all. Of course he has. The detective has made a community call on Samson's wife, to check that she's safe and that he doesn't hurt her. She said he hasn't and doesn't. The detective knows this could potentially be a lie, but at least he checked on her.

He told her to call him if she ever has anything to report. I hope this encourages her to report him if he has been hurting her and the children.

Please protect her and the children, Lord.

July 5th

    I got in contact with the police detective again. He said he didn't think my case would go to court, because Samson denied it all, and it's very hard to find evidence this many years after the fact. It's a bit upsetting and disappointing, but at least the detective is still doing something about it. He hasn't just put my case straight on the shelf after Samson's denial. He believes me, he knows that Samson is still potentially dangerous. He's taking it seriously.

August 1st

    I've been seeing a new psychologist and using cognitive behavioural therapy. I find it helpful to see where in my brain the trauma comes from and where else in my brain it links to.

    We'll work through each trauma and how it's affecting my brain. Then, if I still need more help, we'll do EMDR; a rapid eye movement desensitising therapy that's supposed to work really well.

August 9th

    The psychiatrist asked me about my traumas today, then diagnosed me with complex PTSD, which means the effects of the many traumas have piled on top of each other, compounding them. She upped my pills, which will help. She said she's never seen anyone with complex PTSD so well adapted before, and that I'm doing really well.

    I must now work on believing how awesome I am, and how well I am doing in life and with recovery. A psychiatrist wouldn't say that if it weren't true. And that's four witnesses now; Mum, Timothy, the psychiatrist and a friend, all saying the same thing; that I'm doing remarkably well.

It's about time I expelled the thoughts that tell me I'm stupid, that I'm not doing well.

I am not stupid, useless or a waste of space. I am awesome, I am smart, I am clever, I am talented, I am good, I am useful, I am doing well.

February 2023

I finally reported Uncle Shark for what he did to Candace. I had to give it to the authorities and get it out of my system. I feel so much calmer about it already.

From these selected diary entries, you can see how far I've come, how much I did to help myself heal, how much work has gone into creating positive changes for others.

I'm finally able to believe I'm awesome. I still have more work to do, but I am much better than I was. Sometimes I still have triggers, but they are much less frequent now. I have learned to handle them better.

I've learned that recovery isn't linear. Even when it seems like I've gone backwards for miles, if I look at my recovery journey as a whole, I can see that in reality, I'm getting further and further away from my trauma, and closer and closer to Jesus.

I now know I have forgiven Samson, because I made a choice to forgive him, despite the pain. It's the choice to forgive that counts. My feelings about what he did will change over time. I have learned that strong emotions do not prove a lack of forgiveness. Instead, they prove that I'm human, and that I need to feel to recover.

And I'm still using my gifts to help others.

I have recovered much of myself. Although I still have a long way to go, I can see that I have already recovered confidence, trust in my own judgement, courage, strength, peace, joy and truth.

Joy can be found in even the darkest storms; even amidst deep turmoil and lament.

"The joy of the Lord is our strength." Biblical book of Nehemiah, chapter 8, verse 10.

CHAPTER 43

My Journey Continues:
Looking Forward to the Future

In 2019, we moved to Forest Glen, to a perfect old farmhouse with two fireplaces, a big, fenced off garden and an office each for Timothy and me.

To help me deal with my trauma flashbacks, I took Bree exploring. We found a little waterfall flowing into a local creek, a steep-sided gorge, and a beautiful valley filled with streams, waterfalls and waterholes. Bonding with both nature and my son really helped me.

Then Covid struck and we had to home school for a while. I found regular lessons really difficult, so I took Bree out to local beauty spots instead and taught him in nature. For example, his maths was counting the number of fences in the paddocks. Doing lessons this way really helped us both; him with his learning and me with my mental health.

Worship at the Promised Land Camp

One particular worship week at Promised Land Camp was instrumental in my healing. Paul and Dad had organised a School of the Prophets meeting to be held on the first Saturday.

Dad and Raymond spoke about prophecy, and Paul got us to interact with the teaching via some group worship. Many of the old crew came.

Dad challenged us to go to different waterways in Tasmania and pray over them. After that, Paul spoke about angels gathering around the lake. He asked Lucas to respond to them with his silver trumpet, so Lucas blew it loud and clear across the lake.

Once the session was over, I told Paul I already knew my assignment. I was to kayak across the D'entrecasteaux from Tinderbox to Bruny Island, praying for healing for both places, and for them to be connected together in Christ.

As we were eating dinner and chatting with Theodore, he prophesied about Bree, saying, "There's something about that boy! He is an Elijah." I replied, "I know!"

Only a few minutes later, he had a prophecy for me. He said, "Something happened at 16, and on behalf of all good men, I say sorry. You are loved, you are believed, and you are seen." I felt like his words took the label "slut" off me, something I'd been wearing for years, and we prayed for those labels to stay off me. It was amazing.

After dinner, we kicked off our all-night vigil with spontaneous worship and prayer. Someone talked about dancing in the ballroom with the Lord, then stopped mid-sentence, as though they were unsure of their own word, and worried about it sounding silly. But I knew it was right because I'd had a similar insight. So I played a song on my harp about dancing in the ballroom with the Lord.

People began to intercede, and one woman stood against the abuse of young people in her prayers. She spoke in tongues and I had the interpretation.

As yet, no one had taken the leadership spot for the twelve to one a.m. session, so I said I'd do it. God told me to stay up until twelve anyway, so why not lead that session and stay up till one? It's only an hour longer.

I had no plan for the session, so I asked God to show me how to start. He told me to light a single candle and place it in front of me, then kneel in front of it and pray. I did that, and He said to lead the others in a prayer of repentance, so we could begin from a place of humility.

Then I gave God the session and asked him to lead it.

We sat quietly for a while, until I heard God say, "Give me your backpacks!"

I spoke briefly about what that meant, then I began playing a song about it on my harp. Partway through, I felt that Josie ought to play along with me on the piano. She agreed and we played together, following one another in the song.

The musical momentum grew until it got to a place where I felt free to sing about us giving God our backpacks. After a while, the song changed to become a song about letting God give us a new backpack full of blessings. I started urging others to give God their old backpacks and take hold of their new ones as gifts from Him.

The congregation didn't respond how I thought they should, so I stopped playing music and began listening to them instead. (This is a good plan, people!)

I shared about my own backpacks first. I told them that my whole life, I'd been carrying a backpack of shame that wasn't mine; that it had been put on me by Samson. Then I shared how April had previously helped me lay that one down and take up my new one from Father. It's blue with a rainbow on it, and inside is more freedom, more joy and more of Him.

Josie said her small "Dora the Explorer" backpack just had water in it, because she needed to trust the Lord to provide for her. April suggested that as Dora is a children's show, this was linked to Josie needing to learn to have a childlike faith.

April shared that there was joy in her backpack.

Then Michelle said she felt like it was going to take a lot of work to get her old backpack off. It was stuck and she didn't know why. I said it was OK if she couldn't get it off straight away; that it would come off in time if she kept working with Jesus.

Amber had tools and a grappling hook in hers. She said she felt like God wanted her to go to new heights, and he'd given her the tools to do so. As Josie and I were praying for the last two women, Theodore, Lucas and Timothy arrived for the next session. They sat down to join us, and were surprised by the amount of joy in the room. We were all smiling and laughing.

In the previous session, it had all been about the lament. And then the joy came! God always has a plan and it's always good.

Such good memories. Such good times with God. Promised Land, a place where everyone is free to be themselves, and a place of healing. My times there really helped me move on from my trauma and begin to heal, to celebrate who I am in Christ, to love myself and to feel proud of my contributions.

Agent of Change

I believe God allowed me to have that really intense period of traumatic memory so that I could get it out of my system and finally begin to heal. I don't make excuses for any of the perpetrators anymore. I no longer tell myself (or others) that it wasn't that bad. I have seen the truth and the truth continues to set me free. I am not going to lie to myself anymore, or sugar coat the abuse to make others feel comfortable.

Having a psychotherapist listen to me without judgement was exactly what I needed, it allowed me to move forward. And my loved ones were really supportive, which was a great help too. (Shout out to Timothy, Mum, Breanna, Josie and Louana.) Writing has been another Godsend. Just letting the words flow out of me creatively has been so important for my healing journey.

I have also learned that my pain is worth something. It is not pointless or hopeless. Some good has already come out of it. God is using my story, and my willingness to share it, to help others. My story has inspired other women to open up about their trauma, and to seek their own healing. My courage has given them courage.

And through this, God has deepened me in my ability to listen without judgement, and in my capacity to extend grace. I believe it's this ability to show grace that's enabled others to tell me about their struggles; they know I won't judge them, and I'll do what I can to help them.

Talking about such things had to start somewhere, and praise God that within my community, it started with me.

I have also corresponded with several politicians, asking for law reform in sexual assault and domestic violence laws, and I've written to my old school asking for an apology. All of these were met with positive results. I received an apology from the education department, on behalf of my old school, and I've heard back from several of the politicians I wrote to. One forwarded my letter on to the attorney general and the other outlined to me the changes she is already making in these matters.

I continue to pray for law reform. Will you pray with me?

God is using me as a change maker, a forerunner. Thank you, God, for taking this girl and making her into your warrior princess. Look out world, here I come!

HELPFUL ORGANISATIONS

Here is a list of organisations and references which may be helpful for trauma survivors and their families.

National Sexual Assault Support with Respect.gov.au: 24hr help line: 1800 737 732.

Bravehearts; an organisation that supports abused children: www.bravehearts.org.au

1800 Respect (1800 737 732) A national helpline for victims of domestic violence.

Each Australian state has its own sexual assault support services. Here is a list by state:

Tasmania
Sexual Assault Support Services (SASS):
- 24 hr crisis support: 1800 697 877
- All other enquiries: (03) 6231 0044

Laurel House, Launceston:
- (03) 6334 2740
- Burnie/Devonport offices: (03) 6431 9711

- Crisis Line: 1800 697 877

Victoria
Sexual Assault Crisis Line Victoria: 1800 806 292
Centres against Sexual Assault Central Victoria: (03) 5441 0430
Victorian Women's Health Services: (03) 9664 9300

New South Wales
NSW Rape Crisis Counselling Service: 1800 424 017

Australian Capital Territory
Canberra Rape Crisis Centre: (02) 6247 2525
Service Assisting Male Survivors of Sexual Assault: (02) 6247 2525

Queensland
Sexual Assault Helpline: 1800 010 120
DV Connect Men's Line counselling service for male victims: 1800 600 636

Northern Territory
Sexual Assault Referral Centres:
- Darwin (08) 8922 6472
- Alice Springs (08) 8955 4500
- Katherine (08) 8973 8524
- Tennant Creek (08) 8962 4361

Western Australia
- **Sexual Assault Resource Centre (SARC):** (08) 6458 1828
- **Crisis Line 1800 199 888**

South Australia:
Yarrow Place:
- 24 hr line: 1800 817 421

Helpful Websites

Lifeline: www.lifeline.org.au Counsellors are available 24/7 for people who feel suicidal. Help is also available by phone: 131 114

Reach Out: www.au.reachout.com A website that lists information about domestic abuse, sexual assault and mental health. Online counselling and support chat groups are available.

www.eatingdisorderhope.com

www.butterfly.org.au

You can also call the National Eating Disorder Association America: (212) 575 6200 or checkout their website: www.nationaleatingdisorders.org

Help is available and you are not alone. You matter, you are seen, you are believed and you are loved.

FURTHER READING

On the Topic of Spirit Sexual Abuse:
From theparanormalchronicles.com: "An excerpt from 'Ghost Sex: The Violation'"
From New Vison: (www.newvision.co.ug), "Raped by Demons"
From Research Gate: (www.researchgate.net), "The Young Female Body as a Site of Demonic Sexual Abuse: The Case of Christians in Charismatic Pentecostal Churches in Durban, South Africa"
An account on Reddit: (amp.reddit.com search for succubus)
"Sexuality in Christian Demonology", an article on Wikipedia
"Incubus", an article on Wikipedia
"Succubus", an article on Wikipedia
"Sleep Paralysis", an article on Wikipedia
"The Phenomenon of Spirit Sexual Abuse," a soon to come book by Jules Green

On the Topic of Rape, Assault, Sexual Harassment and Domestic Violence:
The documentary, "The Hunting Ground," first released February 2015, Sundance Films
The documentary, "Slut or Nut: The Diary of a Rape Trial," first released May 2018, Journeyman Pictures

From www.theconversation.com an article entitled, "Rape, Sexual Assault and Sexual Harassment: What's the Difference?"

From www.au.rechout.com an article entitled, "What is Sexual Assault?"

From www.self.com an article entitled, "What is Sexual Assault (and What Isn't) According to Law."

A booklet called, "Red Flags," published by the Huon Domestic Violence Service, 2020

"See What You Made Me Do," a book by Jess Hill, published 2020, and the subsequent mini-series on SBS

"The Beauty of Consent and the Reality of Rape," a soon to come book by Jules Green

On the Topic of Predatory Behaviour and Personality Disorders:

"How to spot a sexual predator – the 8 characteristics," from www.healthista.com

An article entitled, "The Thinking Processes of Sexual Predators," from www.psychologytoday.com

An article entitled, "What is Grooming? Signs to Look Out For," from www.bark.us

An article entitled, "Signs of Grooming in Adults – What to Watch Out For," from www.anncrafttrust.org

An article entitled, "How to Spot a Sexual Predator: Psychologist Breaks Down 8 Classic Warning Signs and How to Protect Yourself," from www.dailymail.co.uk

An article entitled, "In the Mind of a Sexual Offender," from www.hopeandsafety.org

An article entitled, "What is a Psychopath?" from www.health-line.com

An article entitled, "Understanding Psychopathic Tendencies," from www.tsemrinpoche.com

An article entitled, "Worried You Are Dating a Psychopath? Signs to Look For," from www.theconversation.com

An article entitled, "Eight Possible Signs of Psychopathic Tendencies," from www.psychologytoday.com

An article entitled, "Stages of the Psychopathic Bond" from www.psycopathsandlove.com

On the Topic of Good Relationships and Abusive Relationships, and How to Tell the Differences:

"10 Signs a Guy Respects You," an article on www.make-himyours.com.au

"8 Signs You're With Someone Who Respects You," in a Bustle magazine article, (www.bustle.com)

"Healthy Relationships: A Biblical Guide for Young People" A soon to come book by Jules Green

"Stalking" a soon to come book by Jules Green

On the Topic of Healthy Body Image:

An article entitled, "Eating Disorders – Causes, Types and Treatments" on www.healthdirect.gov.au

"Healthy Body Image" a soon to come book by Jules Green

On the Topic of Marriage and Waiting:

"Captivating" a book by Stassi Eldridge, first published 2005 by Nelson Books

From the Bible:

- Matthew 19: 3-9
- Genesis chapters 1-3
- Proverbs chapters 1-2 and chapter 31

- Song of Songs chapter 3

An article entitled "Want More and Better Sex? Get Married and Stay Married" on www.huffpost.com

"Poll Shows Sex within Marriage is More Fulfilling" on www.imom.com

"What's going on with Hormones and Neurotransmitters During Sex?" on www.atlasbiomed.com

"Healthy Sexuality: A Biblical Guide for Young People" a soon to come book by Jules Green

On the Topic of Healing from Trauma:

"How to Heal the Traumatised Brain" on www.psychologytoday.com

"The Brain that Changes Itself", a book by Norman Doidge, MD

"How to Rewire Your Traumatised Brain" on www.nytimes.com

"Generalised Anxiety Disorder – Symptoms and Causes" on www.mayoclinic.org

"Post-Traumatic Stress Disorder (PTSD) – Information and Resources" on www.blackdoginstitute.org.au

"The 5 Types of PTSD" on the psych2go you tube channel

"Researchers reveal the 6 responses to stress" on www.dailymail.co.uk

"There are more F's to flight, fight and freeze" on www.enlightenedsolutions.com

"Freezing during Sexual Assault and Harassment" on www.psychologytoday.com.au

"How Trauma Affects the Brain: Doctor's Notes" on www.torontostar.com

"Why Understanding Why a Child's Brain Works at Different Stages is so Important" on www.independent.co.uk

"Brain Development in Children" on www.startingblocks.gov.au

"When the Brain Starts Adulating" on www.brainfacts.org

"You Can Heal: A Book about Trauma Recovery," a soon to come book by Jules Green

"Learning to Forgive" a soon to come book by Jules Green

ACKNOWLEDGMENTS

I want to thank first and foremost God, Jesus and Holy Spirit, who have kept me alive through many scary situations. I truly may be dead if not for you!

Thank you to my awesome husband Timothy, who has shown me what a good man is, what a healthy relationship is, and what respect in romance looks like. I am so blessed to have him!

To Bree: thank you for putting up with moody, distressed Mummy; doing her best but struggling. Thank you for loving me anyway.

Thanks to my sister Breanna for putting up with difficult phone calls, and for helping me through the memories; sometimes just with a listening ear, other times with a sleepover, a walk in the bush and some drinks. Breanna, you are truly special.

Thanks to Mum, who listened to my experiences with horror, and actually named what I went through as horrific; the first person other than me to admit that it was. Thank you for not sugar coating your own feelings about it and for not pretending everything was alright. Your ability to be real with me helped me be real with myself. You are the best Mum ever!

Thanks Dad, for always talking sense to me.

Thanks to my best friends Josie, Dahlia and Louana, who listened while I sorted myself out. Thanks for being there for me.

Thanks to my awesome older prayer warriors; the ones I always call for prayer support when times are tough: Marigold, Angela, Auntie Edwina, Champion and Wanda. You guys are awesome! Marigold, you are like an auntie to me. Angela, you are like a spiritual Grandma to me, always protecting, always encouraging, and always with a great strategy to offer; one of the most trustworthy people I know. Champion, you are like a spiritual grandma too. Wanda thank you for your wisdom. And Edwina, you *are* my auntie! I appreciate you all.

Thanks to those who had my back when I made the difficult but necessary decision to report Samson to the police, and to write necessary complaint letters. I'm glad I did it. Look at the results!

Thanks to Jacquie Petrusma for replying to my letter and for caring. Not many other politicians did.

Thanks to my bosses for helping me out and for understanding my needs. You guys are great, the best employers ever!

Finally, thank you to the Riverton Café for allowing me to sit and write this book, even when I was in tears; for seeing me jumpy and scared without judgement, and for loving me anyway.

I hope you all enjoyed this book. Remember, if any of your own traumas were raised, there are counsellors and psychotherapists available. You can also try local churches or GPs.

Please refer to the helpful organisations section of this book to find crisis contacts, and to the further reading section for helpful reads. I wish you all the best through your own healing journey!

Thank you for reading,
Sincerely,
Jules Green.

Breanna holding baby me 1982

Little me

Breanna and I at dog on Tuckerbox, Gundagai

family portrait 1990

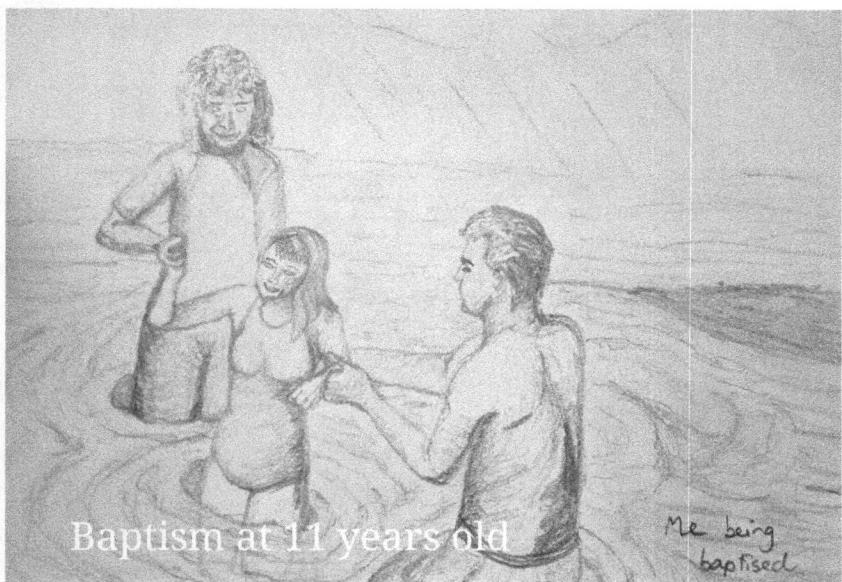
Baptism at 11 years old

Me being baptised

At Twelve Apostles 1999

Breanna   Candace   Dad   Me   JG

Best Friends

www.ingramcontent.com/pod-product-compliance
Lightning Source LLC
Chambersburg PA
CBHW060456090426
42735CB00011B/2001